T0207051

The Web Accessibility Project

The Web Accessibility Project
Development and Testing Best Practices

Narayanan Palani

CRC Press
Taylor & Francis Group
Boca Raton London New York

CRC Press is an imprint of the
Taylor & Francis Group, an **informa** business

AN AUERBACH BOOK

First edition published 2023
by CRC Press
6000 Broken Sound Parkway NW, Suite 300, Boca Raton, FL 33487-2742

and by CRC Press
4 Park Square, Milton Park, Abingdon, Oxon, OX14 4RN

© 2023 Taylor & Francis Group, LLC

CRC Press is an imprint of Taylor & Francis Group, LLC

ISBN: 978-1-032-28083-7 (hbk)
ISBN: 978-1-032-20200-6 (pbk)
ISBN: 978-1-003-29943-1 (ebk)

DOI: 10.1201/9781003299431

Typeset in Garamond
by MPS Limited, Dehradun

This book is dedicated to my dad and mum, Palani and Latha.

Contents

About the Author

Narayanan Palani is an (quality) engineering lead in a major financial institution in the United Kingdom, leading a number of teams across different countries on test automation, accessibility, performance, and security testing interventions. Narayanan has certifications from Microsoft, Scaled Agile, DevOps Institute, International Software Testing Qualifications Board, International Software Quality Institute, with an MS in Software Engineering, Executive MBA, and a certificate of specialisation in Leadership and Management from Harvard Business School Online. His online courses are subscribed by at least 35,000+ students across 158+ countries worldwide and he is currently providing video sessions through engineers-hub. teachable.com. Narayanan is the author of book series "Software Automation Testing Secrets Revealed" and receiver of "Best Test Manager of the Year" award at the European Software Testing Awards, Year 2019. His latest contributions resulted in "Best Agile Project" award in 2021[1] due to the key "Accessibility First" Test approach on web and mobile development platforms.

Note

1. Title: Winners 2021. (Accessed 12 December 2021). Retrieved from https://www.softwaretestingnews. co.uk/products/testawards/winners-2021/

Chapter 1

Introduction

The book you are reading right now is the result of nearly 5 years of my work as an Accessibility Evangelist by implementing digital accessibility using different testing tools that resulted in four different European Software Testing awards during 2018–2021[1]. By applying the accessibility best practices I teach you in this book, you will experience an explosive results in your work and help your organization rise to a whole new level of accessibility adherence, innovation, and inclusive design. You will also gain greater work satisfaction in your life by helping improve digital accessibility for your end users. This book helps with some of the readily usable best practices to adapt web accessibility early in application development and attract potential job opportunities in leading organizations internationally.

Around 26%–29% of C-Suite executives and Digital Accessibility decision-makers in the United Kingdom shared their views that they lack internal skills and experience as a barrier for delivering digital accessibility[2]. Hence building accessibility skillset through books and internal training programs is essential to enhance digital accessibility awareness across engineering teams. Now that you're started to reading this wonderful book, let me thank you for your wonderful ambition to make a positive impact on people's life through better accessibility. If you think your professional network can be benefited from reading best practices from this book, please feel free to share the book reviews through Linkedin, Twitter, Facebook, Instagram, and other social media channels. Your positive spread of accessibility awareness will definitely give a boost to people around you to learn about accessibility to make it a better and inclusive world for everyone.

Ambition

Approximately 15% of the global population is affected by some sort of disability[3] as per the World Report on Disability. Based on recent survey from AbilityNet[4], 22% of C-Suite executives perceive digital accessibility (DA) as a "never-ending task" among the survey participants. Among the engineering leaders, one in four leaders are reliant on very less (limited) knowledge about DA. Since global collective of 500 CEOs and their organizations signed up to commit and bring disability on their leadership agenda part of The Valuable 500[5], the opportunities to learn and adapt digital accessibility is very niche and new jobs are being created everyday across different countries to know and implement "accessibility" as a mandatory skill rather than a competitive advantage.

Most of the countries are increasing their legislative efforts to make web accessibility an important part in web development and testing of software releases. On the other hand, many organizations are facing extreme turbulence when not adhering to international accessibility guidelines while developing their software's and website applications[6]. Web Content Accessibility Guidelines (WCAG[7]) is a world renowned guideline of accessibility recommendations, which is developed through the W3C process to help organizations meet the minimum standard accessibility guidelines and it has become critical for every organization to focus on implementing the accessibility checks at every stage of their application development to avoid unaffordable mistakes.

Meanwhile it is important for front-end engineers and Quality Assurance (QA) test analysts to adhere to WCAG best practices for efficiently adapting to steps required to incorporate accessibility focused inclusive design, development and extensive accessibility testing are essential for most of the customer-facing websites. In a fast-paced world, incorporating shift left accessibility within development and testing is the new normal and this book helps developers address right accessibility attributes to UI components and focus on developing manual and automation tests for QA professionals to inject accessibility audit, accessibility functional tests, and accessibility automation tests part of their Continuous Integration and Continuous Development (CI/CD) models.

In short, disability impacts everyone in life and almost 70% of disabilities are invisible,[8] hence the need to adhere to guidelines and adopt websites to help users with disabilities is mission critical while delivering software applications. When target users access websites with invisible disabilities,[9] they use assistive technologies to access websites, such as screen readers, zooming text tools, or alternative mechanism to interact with websites. So test automation is not an end goal of accessibility tests and majority of the accessibility checks need to be done through screen reader and assistive technology interactions (in addition to automated tests and scans), hence the following steps of scanning the web application (SCAN) followed by series of screen reader/zoom/color-based tests (SCREEN READ) and automate part of the tests through test automation tools (AUTOMATE) are better ways of strategizing web accessibility tests through "SCAN-SCREEN-READ-AUTOMATE FRAMEWORK."

The ambition of this book is to help you elegantly reach your absolute best by implementing web accessibility best practices through Scan-ScreenRead-Automate to help everyone around you.

Guidelines

Web Content Accessibility Guidelines (WCAG)[10], Authoring Tool Accessibility Guidelines (ATAG)[11], User Agent Accessibility Guidelines (UAAG),[12] and Accessible Rich Internet Applications (WAI-ARIA)[13] are most frequently used accessibility guidelines[14] to compare and follow the international guidelines to adapt best practices. I have visited at least 300 developers and testers in the past 4 years (before COVID-19 pandemic) and most of them had a WCAG Reference Guide[15] on their office walls and desk spaces to refer to the guidelines and compare when defects are identified. If you are beginning to learn web accessibility, it is highly recommended to use WCAG cheat sheets and reference guides for reference while testing the websites. Most of the WCAG guidelines are classified under four key principles,[16] namely Robust,

Operable, Perceivable, and Understandable, hence I request readers to refer the latest WCAG version from w3.org time to time.

Scope

This book refers to WCAG version 2.1[17] and version 2.2 to provide best examples from author's experience across different websites, and readers are recommended to use screen readers such as NVDA (or JAWS alternatively) while performing web accessibility tests as recommended in each chapter. There may be developments and better solutions available in the near future for similar problems discussed in this book, hence readers are advised to refer to latest WCAG guidelines, government regulations to follow right suitable tests in their target websites for testing. Occasionally, few mistakes are possible while explaining the test automation code in this book in which users are recommended to post the issues in open source GitHub repositories to rectify any code issues.

First part of this book talks about different examples of defects pertaining to websites ranging from page title, heading to latest challenges like single page application's accessibility issues by narrating through fictional characters who are part of web accessibility project to implement best practices. Second part of this book talks about Cypress testing automation tool in which different essential test techniques can be implemented to evaluate web accessibility using plugins and test tricks.

Readers are expected to have

- Minimum 1–4 years of HTML5 experience and some development experience (preferably any front end application development such as JavaScript, React, etc.)
- Minimum 1–4 years of experience in any Quality Assurance(QA) roles
- Some knowledge on JavaScript to develop and test using tools such as CypressIO

Screen Reader Recommendations

While reading each chapter of this book, readers are recommended to use NVDA[18] screen reader on your target websites to test corresponding web components for better hands-on experience. NVDA is a popular screen reader and is widely used as an open source screen reader for Windows laptops and desktops.

While writing this book, NVDA has 30% usage across the respondents to the survey of year 2021 at webaim.org; it may be possible that new screen readers emerge and percentage changes over a period of time, hence requesting to choose alternative screen readers based on the latest survey results.[19]

Open Source Code Repositories

Author has provided several open source projects to support the readers through his GitHub open source initiatives[20] and "Web Accessibility Test Cases"[21] are one of the most used manual test cases for web accessibility test needs; similarly two Cypress frameworks are constructed and provided free using "Cypress Test Techniques"[22] and "Cypress API Test Techniques"[23] repositories. It is the user's responsibility to perform adequate security scans and vulnerability checks on the open source code base since author is not responsible for maintaining these free-to-use, open source repositories due to limitations in handling the code contribution from contributors across the world.

OrangeHRM[24] is an open source application, free software used to represent the accessibility test implementations using WAVE, CypressIO, and other tools across this book and readers are requested to launch their demo website to login[25] and experience the features if required.

Disclaimer

Even though the author has tried to provide best possible examples in each accessibility issues in different scenarios, the author is not responsible for any scenario gaps during the accessibility testing implementation as this book is not an official guide to any testing tool and this book may not be referred as an official guide for accessibility testing. The primary objective of this book is to provide versatile examples to software developers and testers to help them in learning the needs and usage of test tools and techniques. Under no circumstances will the author be held responsible or liable in any way for any claims, damages, losses, expenses, costs, or liabilities whatsoever (including, without limitation, any direct or indirect damages for loss of profits, business interruption, or loss of information) resulting or arising directly or indirectly from your use of or inability to use this book or websites discussed in this book or any websites linked to it, or from your reliance on the information and material on this book, even if the author has advised of the possibility of such damages in advance.

Please note: sometime books may not be the only mode of learning for particular group of accessibility implementation hence interested candidates can watch the videos online at teachable[26], IAPP.org[27], Deque University[28] on different web accessibility courses that are independent to this book.

Notes

1. Best Use of Technology in a Project-Year 2018, The (Overall) European Software Testing Award -Year 2018, Best Testing Manager of the Year 2019, Best Agile Project of the Year 2021-European Testing Awards. (Accessed 12 December 2021). Retrieved from https://www.softwaretestingnews.co.uk/products/testawards/
2. Title: What do C-Suite leaders think about digital accessibility? (Accessed 12 December 2021). Retrieved from https://abilitynet.org.uk/news-blogs/what-do-c-suite-leaders-think-about-digital-accessibility
3. Title: Disability: The global picture. (Accessed 12 December 2021). Retrieved from https://humanity-inclusion.org.uk/
4. Title: What do C-Suite leaders think about digital accessibility? (Accessed 12 December 2021). Retrieved from https://abilitynet.org.uk/news-blogs/what-do-c-suite-leaders-think-about-digital-accessibility
5. Title: Valuable 500. (Accessed 12 December 2021). Retrieved from https://www.thevaluable500.com/about
6. Title: Title III Lawsuits: 10 Big Companies Sued Over Website Accessibility. (Accessed 12 December 2021). Retrieved from https://www.essentialaccessibility.com/blog/title-iii-lawsuits-10-big-companies-sued-over-website-accessibility
7. Title: W3C Accessibility Standards Overview. (Accessed 12 December 2021). Retrieved from https://www.w3.org/WAI/standards-guidelines/
8. Title: Linkedin Post from Accidental Ally. (Accessed 12 December 2021). Retrieved from https://www.linkedin.com/posts/gkini_accessibiltymatters-theaccidentalally-kudos-activity-6833800956149415936-_eiW

9. Title: Beneath The Surface – A closer look at invisible disabilities. (Accessed 12 December 2021). Retrieved from https://theaccidentalally.com/toolkit/accessibility-personas/
10. Title: Web Content Accessibility Guidelines (WCAG). (Accessed 12 December 2021). Retrieved from https://www.w3.org/WAI/standards-guidelines/#wcag2
11. Title: Authoring Tool Accessibility Guidelines (ATAG). (Accessed 12 December 2021). Retrieved from https://www.w3.org/WAI/standards-guidelines/#atag
12. Title: User Agent Accessibility Guidelines (UAAG). (Accessed 12 December 2021). Retrieved from https://www.w3.org/WAI/standards-guidelines/#uaag
13. Title: Accessible Rich Internet Applications (WAI-ARIA). (Accessed 12 December 2021). Retrieved from https://www.w3.org/TR/wai-aria-1.1/
14. Title: W3C Accessibility Standards Overview. (Accessed 12 December 2021). Retrieved from https://www.w3.org/WAI/standards-guidelines/
15. Title: WCAG 2.1 Map. (Accessed 12 December 2021). Retrieved from http://intopia.digital/pdf/WCAG2_1Map.pdf
16. Title: Understanding the Four Principles of Accessibility. (Accessed 12 December 2021). Retrieved from https://www.w3.org/TR/UNDERSTANDING-WCAG20/intro.html
17. Title: WCAG 2.1 at a Glance. (Accessed 12 December 2021). Retrieved from https://www.w3.org/WAI/WCAG21/Techniques/css/C30.html
18. Title: NV Access. (Accessed 12 December 2021). Retrieved from https://www.nvaccess.org/
19. Screen Reader User Survey #9 Results. (Accessed 12 December 2021). Retrieved from https://webaim.org/projects/screenreadersurvey9/
20. Title: Hello, I am Narayanan Palani. (Accessed 12 December 2021). Retrieved from https://github.com/narayananpalani
21. Title: webAccessibilityTestCases. (Accessed 12 December 2021). Retrieved from https://github.com/narayananpalani/webAccessibilityTestCases
22. Title: Cypress Test Techniques. (Accessed 12 December 2021). Retrieved from https://github.com/narayananpalani/cypress-test-techniques
23. Title: Cypress API Test Techniques. (Accessed 12 December 2021). Retrieved from https://github.com/narayananpalani/cypress-api-test-techniques
24. Title: OrangeHRM Open Source Application-Free to use under the GNU General Public License. (Accessed 12 December 2021). Retrieved from https://github.com/orangehrm/orangehrm
25. Title: OrangeHRM Open Source Application Login Page. (Accessed 12 December 2021). Retrieved from https://opensource-demo.orangehrmlive.com/
26. Engineers Hub. (Accessed 12 December 2021). Retrieved from https://engineers-hub.teachable.com/
27. Title: IAPPCertification. (Accessed 12 December 2021). Retrieved from https://iapp.org/certify/free-study-guides/
28. Title: Digital Accessibility Courses & Accessibility Reference Library. (Accessed 12 December 2021). Retrieved from https://dequeuniversity.com/

Chapter 2

Web Accessibility Basics

What is Web Accessibility?

Web Accessibility is a very important best practice to improve the usability of websites, hence users with disabilities of some sort will make use of it when accessing. Approximately 20% of global population belong to these special users' category who need assistive technologies to access websites, such as contact lenses and screen readers (e.g., JAWS, NVDA). Since technology is meant for everyone, applications should be developed by having accessibility in mind.

Most of us face some sort of vision problems with aging, hence accessibility is for everyone. Visual disabilities such as color blindness, low vision, partial or full blindness are just some of the disabilities. Users with hearing disabilities, such as partial hearing loss or deafness also needs to be addressed with better accessibility when accessing websites. Physical disabilities such as motor control diseases and speech challenges also hinder users' abilities and hence they opt for assistive technologies to access websites. In addition to all these type of disabilities, cognitive disabilities such as learning disabilities, distractibility or inability to recollect memory, or inability to focus are some of the most common disabilities that need better accessibility features.

Even a father holding his new-born in one hand and trying to book medical appointment on his mobile phone web browser needs better accessibility to quickly access the website and book the medical appointment. Similarly, temporary disabilities such as intermediate hospital admissions due to injury or surgery hinder our ability to use websites for some important activities, such as booking cabs through website or book meals. Overall, these disabilities are of variable degrees and mostly in combinations such as a user who has 60% vision loss with hearing problems. Similarly, if a user is 100% hearing impaired, he or she may also be suffering from some sort of motor disease in addition. Hence, to cater to diversified customers with different disabilities is the key objective while building the websites. These visual, physical, speech, auditory, cognitive disabilities get worse over time, hence we need to carefully build applications that give users better experience along with assistive technologies.

Visual Disabilities

If you are using contact lenses or glasses to see websites, it is also a form of visual disability due to low vision. It can be correctable or irreversible vision loss in either one or both the eyes. People

DOI: 10.1201/9781003299431-2

with color blindness and vision loss rely on features such as zoom font size, color, and spacing most of the time. Audio description of the video is must for these types of disabilities to help them read through text-to-speech screen readers, such as JAWS, NVDA, etc.

Lessons Learnt: Users should use their custom settings, such as zoom font size or read through text-to-speech screen readers without any major problems while accessing the websites. It is most common to see a video with no audio description available in few websites—this is one of the most common barriers for users with disabilities. Similarly, missing text alternatives or incorrect labelling or missing captions or transcripts for any form of video or audio, poor or inconsistent navigation, color-based orientation cues (hence users with color blindness cannot differentiate them) are some of the most common disabilities or challenges in websites while testing against web accessibility.

Hearing Disabilities

Everyone at some point face problems with hearing aging. Loss of hearing is the most common disability and website-based videos are to be provided with audio description, which are the transcripts that can be provided with font size and color-adjusting possibilities, hence those users may also have the combination of visual impairments to some extent. If the video background has some noise, it is challenging in understanding the content, hence video with no background noise is essential.

Sign language is a common method of communicating for people with hearing disabilities. Please take time to watch one of the YouTube videos on sign language, which will help you to understand the need to enhance SPA websites with sign languages whenever appropriate: https://www.youtube.com/watch?v=CnL4USny6tQ. Similarly "Digital accessible information system" is a technical standard to publish your digital websites or any digital documents in audio books or periodicals to help users with disabilities, hence these audio substitutes help users to learn from mp3 or xml formatted files to search, place bookmarks, and help in better navigation. The following page will help learning on DAISY: https://openlibrary.org/help/faq/accessing

Learning, Cognitive, Neurological, and Hidden & Unnoticed Disabilities

When websites are built with better accessibility, it has to be tested against various combinations of disabilities in mind, such as:

- Attention Deficit Hyperactivity Disorder (ADHD): Users with trouble in focusing
- Autism
- Down syndrome (intellectual disabilities)
- Depression, mental health disabilities
- Memory impairments
- Diseases like Multiple Sclerosis (MS), dyslexia, migraine
- Seizure disabilities like epilepsy

The following are the general barriers to be kept in mind during building a website:

- Complex phrases or wordings
- Flashing animation or moving contents (Refer 2.3.1 **Three Flashes or Below Threshold of WCAG Guidelines)**
- No options provided to users to stop/pause/disable those animations or moving contents
- Audio of a media which will not allow users to turn it off/on/pause

Speech Disabilities

When normal speech is interrupted with communication disorders, "Voice Recognition" options or "Voice Recording" options in the websites are needed as alternatives for assistance. Users with stammering disorder, Dysarthria (slow speech with limited tongue), or Alalia (speech delay) need a feature alternative when "voice recognition" mechanism is used.

Major problems with few of the websites are that the contact option is provided with telephone number most of the time. But this is not sufficient for users with speech disability since they need an alternative contact option, such as an email or postal address to send letters or different form of contact options other than voice communication.

Even if your telephone line contains an automated call handler to receive questions and answer automatically, it will be extremely difficult for users with speech disability since they can't pronounce most of the times.

Physical Disabilities

When users suffer from different physical conditions like joint disorders, chronic pain, broken limbs, paralysis, or any diseases that limit the control of their muscles, they need better accessibility until they recover.

Majority of these affected users try accessing websites through ergonomic keyboard or specially made accessibility keyboards or mouse that enable them to perform actions, such as type, click, enter, etc.

Some users are provided with mouth stick or head pointer devices to interact with websites and some use voice recognition software. You may recollect that one of the famous scientists uses an eye-tracking device to interact with the websites as he was suffering with mobility diseases. Text-to-speech screen readers are the most common tools that are used by users with disabilities in majority of the countries and both JAWS and NVDA are leading screen readers that provide text-to-speech assistance. When using mobile phone, voiceover is used in IOS devices and Talkback is used in Android devices.

Following are the most common barriers for users with physical disability:

- Limited time is provided to perform action like flight booking or hospital appointment, reservations, etc.
- Small clickable areas to perform actions where it will be difficult to zoom and try clicking on small area

- Website without skip navigation links (so user is bound to come across the complete header and tabs to reach to main content after several user actions)
- Website not provided with clear indication of where the current focus is. Similarly, not announcing the current page indication when multiple pages are listed.
- Not providing clear narration on the error description and the navigation, making users start the website actions from the beginning when particular input is invalid. For example, asking user to resubmit the complete form from the beginning when only hospital appointment-based text field has been filled incorrectly.

Laws and Policies Across the Globe

Readers are requested to refer to latest government legislations[2] from respective countries to learn about latest requirements to adhere to government guidelines; while writing this book during 2021, I share here some very important policies for information purpose:

United States: The Americans with Disabilities Act (ADA)
United Kingdom: The Equality Act 2010
Europe: EN 301 549: "Accessibility requirements suitable for public procurement of ICT products and services in Europe"
Canada: Web Standards for the Government of Canada, The Accessibility for Ontarians with Disabilities Act (AODA)

This is not a complete list and readers are requested to establish the scope of the customer base and target countries to read government guidelines from respective countries to adhere to their accessibility standards.

Screen Reader Usage Best Practices

Users with partial or full vision impairment and diseases who face difficulties in seeing a computer use screen readers,[3] such as NVDA or JAWS in Windows computers, Voice Over setup of MacBook and iPhones, and also Talkback for Android when using mobile and tablet devices of Android models.

When developers and testers are trying to use assistive technologies to interact with websites (just like users with disabilities), it is evident that NVDA and JAWS screen readers are really helpful in announcing the web components to detect any early defects from web applications. It is highly recommended to use NVDA keyboard shortcuts[4] while using NVDA screen reader. Alternatively, JAWS screen reader can be used to interact with web applications by following and using the keyboard shortcuts[5] of JAWS Screen Reader.

Engineers trying to test Mac or iPhone-based user behaviors are recommended to follow latest Reference Guides of Voice Over[6] to mimic the user behaviors; similarly, while testing on Android mobile phones, Talkback Reference Guides[7] are really useful and highly recommended to following user interactions, such as swipe left, right, or touch, etc.

Assistive Technologies to Zoom Websites and their Best Practices

Users with partial vision loss receive help from zooming-assist technologies, such as ZoomText[8] or Windows Magnifiers[9]. Also, it is worth to note that users with vision impairments try using both zooming tools and screen readers at the same time while interacting with websites, hence engineers are to find a good coverage on verifying web components against relevant assistive technologies for their customer base to uncover defects early on.

We learnt in brief on different disabilities so far and let us talk about different approaches that are being implemented for web accessibility in various organizations and it is purely based on my overall observation after talking to versatile audiences across National Software Testing Conferences, Global Financial Forums, and Virtual Keynote sessions. Some of the accessibility failure models are important be considered to avoid following the same mistakes or shortcomings, hence failures can be prevented while implementing web accessibility technologies.

Accessibility Failure Models

Some organizations choose to include "accessibility" tasks in different ways in their development life cycle. The success depends on when accessibility checks are introduced in the software development life cycle (SDLC). Before starting to know about accessibility techniques, it is essential to learn about "what not to do?" when implementing accessibility standards. It is not wrong but adding accessibility at the wrong time of the development life cycle or implementing incorrectly will result in unnecessary costs toward redesign, rebuild, and re-tests of websites. If readers are interested to understand more on the user landscape and different ways the users interact with others, it is recommended to watch the YouTube video of first deaf blind person who graduated from Harvard Law, Haben Girma,[10] and her best-selling book "Haben: The Deafblind Woman Who Conquered Harvard Law."[11]

"Accessibility is an Afterthought" Model

As a software engineer, if you think to develop and test accessibility feature post-delivery of functional features, it is a key failure model in which majority of the organizations followed this approach and end up changing their entire architecture in later point in time, which led to unnecessary expenses due to incorrect approach.

"Accessibility Test at the End" Model

Many teams develop and test key features and keep their accessibility testing part for the last phase (most likely on their User Acceptance Testing (UAT phase)) and end up blocking their releases due to unresolvable accessibility defects. The primary reason is that some changes needed to undergo functional components and design of the UI itself, hence they end up redesigning their websites after spotting the accessibility defects at the end, which is a proven failure model.

"Accessibility as a Sprint" Model

One of the scrum master gave me the idea of focusing on first few sprints (technically 15 sprints as an example) to develop key features from backlog and spend just one sprint (16th sprint) in the middle of major release to accommodate accessibility features. He ends up adding good number of defects from 16th sprint to the project backlog, hence they thought of completing the project on 25 sprints but ended up spending 45 sprints overall to deliver the final product. Hence this failure model resulted in spending additional cost for 20 more sprints just because of this "Accessibility as a Sprint" Model.

"Accessibility Features by Accessibility Consultants" Model

At least few of the leaders in the IT industry gave this wonderful idea of bringing accessibility consultants to develop those special accessibility features for the website once the basic features are built within the first 25 sprint cycles. Similarly, bring those accessibility testing specialists to test the items once the features for accessibility are complete; however one of the recent implementation of this model amused me for one main reason: "They forgot to think about UI design in the beginning and focused on single page dynamic load website within initial load in the beginning which replace with new contents as and when user scroll down on the page." After the intervention of accessibility consultants, they ended up redesigning the whole page and this time to develop the website in parallel with accessibility consultants with their key recommendations, hence they lost at least 25 sprint worth efforts due to incorrect accessibility implementation at the beginning.

"Accessibility as an Audit Only" Model

While talking to one of the developers of a reputed retail fashion website in a recent testing conference, he mentioned that they do perform regular accessibility audits using a tool on their Jenkins pipeline, hence they are not spending time on manual accessibility tests and going to live earlier as possible. Later I found that they were in a situation to receive multiple incidents logged against their key features, which are not compatible to major screen reader when users tried to purchase the products online. This is a key lesson that reminded me about the failure of "Accessibility as an audit only" model. If he would have included manual accessibility testing cycle with text-to-speech screen readers, it would have saved considerable cost for their organizations. This is a difficult realization after seeing their failure model of accessibility audit implementation.

"Accessibility as a Developer Check" Model

During a recent webinar, the IT head of an organization mentioned that they don't get the website tested by testers on accessibility and they rely fully on development engineers to scan, audit, and test anything against web accessibility. The major problem with this approach is that developers may not test various text-to-speech screen readers and zooming options on how testers usually explore different accessibility tests. Even though it looks to be a working model, getting dedicated accessibility consultants or accessibility QA to perform manual tests is the trustworthy approach in finding real defects on time. Alternatively, it is recommended to get users with disabilities as the accessibility QA to your project to get some real-time experience.

"Accessibility at Live" Model

One of my friends who is also a functional tester with a major consulting company revealed his method of accessibility testing in live application. While cross questioning him on why he missed to do accessibility checks earlier, he said that there was an enormous amount of pressure to deliver the website development work and no one in their small start-up had time to look at the accessibility guidelines. Hence, they went on to release their website first and started receiving real feedback from customers to work toward accessibility whenever the incidents reported related to it. It was such a bizarre experiment in which I don't entertain talking to him on any accessibility ideas anymore, since he got the concept completely wrong.

Accessibility Success Models

We have been discussing about the failure models for a while. Let us discuss about what a success model in accessibility implementations means.

"EAE (Explore Accessibility Everywhere)" Model

At least few of the best rated QAs in my corporate network explore more possibilities to perform accessibility testing earlier in their life cycle. Specifically, reviewing the user stories against WCAG guidelines is one of the key accessibility testing techniques that is extreme shift left method till date. When Epics and User Stories (Requirements Documents alternatively) are reviewed against accessibility guidelines, it gives an opportunity to update "Acceptance Criteria" with relevant WCAG guidelines success criterion, hence the defects can be prevented rather then discovered later in the stages.

"AG (Accessibility Gate)" Model

Performing accessibility tests in each stages, such as design, build, deploy, test (system integration, regression, and user acceptance tests) is key to adopting and holding a dedicated accessibility committee to review the test results at each stage, as a gate keeper will help prevent these defects from entering into next stages.

"C.A.E.R.A (Color, Accessibility Audit, Exploratory Test, and Regression Automation)" Model

Performing color checks when UI design is getting ready and conducting accessibility audits (using tools like AxeDevTools or AxeGuidedTests) when initial page is built by front-end engineer on their laptops are crucial since they provide first-hand defects; post code build and deploy activities, performing accessibility related exploratory tests (against WCAG guidelines) are key to discover defects, which can be reproduced only by manual tests using screen readers or any assistive technologies; post manual tests, automating accessibility attributes such as aria-label, title, href into automation suite help in regular test runs and intimate as and when those semantic structure collapse due to code changes. Hence, C.A.E.R.A model, both AG and CAERA, can be combined while being implemented in advanced agile teams.

So far we discussed about some important best practices on when and where to implement web accessibility checks. Let us start understanding web accessibility best practices through list of user personas from next chapter onward. It is always easy to learn from a practical software project rather than a list of chapters in a book, hence the next couple of chapters will help in describing some project examples from a web accessibility (illusionary) project.

Notes

1. Title: Valuable 500. (Accessed 12 December 2021). Retrieved from https://www.thevaluable500.com/about/impact
2. Title: Web Accessibility Laws & Policies. (Accessed 12 December 2021). Retrieved from https://www.w3.org/WAI/policies/
3. Title: An introduction to screen readers. (Accessed 12 December 2021). Retrieved from https://abilitynet.org.uk/factsheets/introduction-screen-readers
4. Title: Deque Quick Reference Guide: NVDA for Windows Keyboard Commands. (Accessed 12 December 2021). Retrieved from https://media.dequeuniversity.com/courses/generic/testing-screen-readers/2.0/en/docs/nvda-guide.pdf
5. Title: Deque Quick Reference Guide: JAWS for Windows Keyboard Commands. (Accessed 12 December 2021). Retrieved from https://media.dequeuniversity.com/courses/generic/testing-screen-readers/2.0/en/docs/jaws-guide.pdf
6. Title: Deque Quick Reference Guide: VoiceOver for iOS. (Accessed 12 December 2021). Retrieved from https://media.dequeuniversity.com/courses/generic/testing-screen-readers/2.0/en/docs/voiceover-ios-guide.pdf
7. Title: Deque Quick Reference Guide: TalkBack 9.1+ for Android. (Accessed 12 December 2021). Retrieved from https://media.dequeuniversity.com/en/courses/generic/testing-screen-readers/2.0/docs/talkback-guide.pdf
8. Title: ZoomText Quick Reference Guide. (Accessed 12 December 2021). Retrieved from http://www.zoomtext.com/docs/zt9/Z91_QRG_English_US.pdf
9. Title: Use Magnifier to make things on the screen easier to see. (Accessed 12 December 2021). Retrieved from https://support.microsoft.com/en-us/windows/use-magnifier-to-make-things-on-the-screen-easier-to-see-414948ba-8b1c-d3bd-8615-0e5e32204198
10. "An interview with Haben Girma, the first deaf-blind person to graduate from Harvard Law - New Day NW" YouTube video, (duration in 00:12:08). Posted by "KING 5" (Oct 7, 2019), video source: https://www.youtube.com/watch?v=MOw8CgbFiuY
11. Title: Haben: The Deafblind Woman Who Conquered Harvard Law. (Accessed 12 December 2021). Retrieved from https://www.amazon.co.uk/Haben-Deafblind-Woman-Conquered-Harvard/dp/1538728737/

MANUAL WEB ACCESSIBILITY DEVELOPMENT AND TESTING

Chapter 3

User Personas of Web Accessibility Project

How do we ensure that our engineers provide best web accessibility experience to websites? What are the goals, behaviors, skills to introduce/enhance digital accessibility while contributing to software projects? This book explains those web accessibility tricks and techniques part of an illusionary Web Accessibility Project and following are our key contributors to this project. Let us assume that our illusionary organization is SRF Group (not a real name and not representing any real organization).

Naren is an IT Quality Assurance professional at SRF Group who deals in several businesses, including flights and online groceries across the US, the UK, and Europe, and on his first few projects needed strong accessibility testing since every website has to adhere to WCAG guidelines as per the recent legislation.

With the help of his UAT engineer and Accessibility Consultant he realized that accessibility testing needs more hands-on with screen readers and knowledge on guidelines than he ever thought of. With less time, Naren must organize front-end engineers to develop with right accessibility attributes, streamline inter feature team communications, and effectively raise the defects to prevent accessibility defects from leaking to live customer access, since at least 25% of his customer base is impacted by one or other format of disability.

In a fast-paced agile feature team, three types of accessibility tests help kick-starting the accessibility implementation. Readers not only learn how to improve their own website on accessibility features but they will also never view the GUI the same way again.

This small feature team has some brilliant world-class engineers and managers from different countries associated to their business as follows:

Mark C (a.k.a) MC is an illusional front end ReactJS developer persona in this book.
Naren (a.k.a) N is an illusional quality engineer persona.
Juliet Sullivan (a.k.a) Juliet is an illusional **business analyst** who writes the user stories in agile teams in gherkin format (such as As-I-So for Epics and Given-When-Then for User Stories) and she never forgets to include an exclusive Acceptance Criteria to mention about WCAG Success Criterion whenever any relevant change has been made on the web application.

DOI: 10.1201/9781003299431-4

Claire Raven (a.k.a) C is an illusional **engineering lead** responsible for entire release of the web applications and she live with memory loss (Alzheimer's Stage 4). As the disease itself is progressive with time, we expected to see her forgetting many more things in coming years, which we will notice in later part of the book.

Chandrashekar BK (a.k.a) CBK is an illusional user persona who has 70% vision loss and accesses websites using screen reader and zoomtext who also contributes to **User Acceptance Testing** (a.k.a) UAT.

Nicholas T (a.k.a) Nick is an illusional **accessibility consultant** with 100% vision impairment.

Sandhya (a.k.a) Sandy is an illusional user persona who has restricted growth and accesses the website using talkback feature most of the times in her mobile phone. She is the **designer** to all the projects from SRF Group of websites.

John T (a.k.a) J is an illusional user persona who has 80% hearing impairment due to aging factors and accesses the website using voiceover most of the times in his mobile phone. He is also a native French speaking candidate, hence he set up screen readers to read in French by default.

Valarpirai (a.k.a) Valar is an illusional user persona who holds her newborn in her one hand when she accesses her phone to order groceries, nappies, and pharmacy products using her iPhone.

Gunashekaran (a.k.a) Guna is an illusional user persona who has neurological disorder, hence he uses his tongue (occasionally nose) to perform touch actions on the website using special device and hear most of the interactions using screen reading assistive technology built in his wheelchair. Since he is a wheelchair user in the city of Chennai in India. He finds it difficult to commute using public transport for work and purchasing essentials. Hence he fully relies on online purchase most of the times.

Yamini is an illusional user persona who is the **Accessibility Waiver Board Member** internal to their SRF Organization after Claire reviewed atleast 300+ accessibility defects in the first phase of UI development and offered Yamini a Waiver Board Member job to produce preventive measures to the life cycle and help fastening the product life cycle.

In this book, we aim to provide a better website experience for most of the users who have different kind of disabilities (a.k.a) and are differently abled special users.

None of these characters are representing any real person or identity of any sort and the ambition is to highlight some of the important needs for web accessibility while narrating the story of these persona when they were involved in a web accessibility implementation while developing their websites. We discuss those project examples in upcoming chapters.

Before starting any agile project, SRF group produced an Epic (norm used in agile projects to articulate a high-level requirement of a software application development). Let us read it before heading deep dive into technical development:

NEW EPIC ON THE BACKLOG

COMPANY: SRF GROUP

Following Epic has been prioritized by Lab Product Owner to get it implemented in coming sprints and she explained the details through a PI (Program Increment) session to include relevant user stories associated to it to different feature teams.

Epic Title: Adhere to WCAG 2.2 guidelines on the websites getting built and serviced to customers part of SRF Group

Priority:1

Description: As per the accessibility guidelines narrated in Section 508, The Americans with Disabilities Act (ADA), European Accessibility Act (EAA), Web Content Accessibility Guidelines (WCAG), achieve maximum possible accessibility using assistive technologies by adhering to AA level of WCAG guidelines in every web-based application releases of SRF Group.

Scenario

As user need better accessibility to access SRF group of websites

I develop and test applications using WCAG guidelines

So user is provided with best possible features, configurations, and attributes that help in accessing the website using assistive technologies to the level of AA from WCAG 2.2

Acceptance Criteria

- Perform Shift Left-Accessibility focused Design adhering to WCAG2.2 Level AA
- Perform Shift Left-Accessibility focused Development adhering to WCAG2.2 Level AA
- Perform Shift Left-Accessibility focused SIT testing adhering to WCAG2.2 Level AA
- Perform Shift Left -Accessibility focused UAT testing adhering to WCAG2.2 Level AA

If you carefully read the epic, you would have noticed that accessibility has been incorporated in Acceptance Criteria (ACs), which is a miss from many organizations in earlier stage of the web application development. Since ACs miss the coverage of accessibility, many organizations tend to catch up with accessibility checks and at the end of their project releases and incur huge financial loss as a result. Here at SRF, their BA, Juliet S, is extremely intelligent in including their Accessibility Guidelines as one of the criteria for Definition of Done (DOD) in agile projects.

Now let us look at our tester Naren's interests on WAVE—web accessibility evaluation tool in the next chapter.

Chapter 4

WAVE Evaluation Tool as Accessibility Extension

WAVE is a publicly available extension for Chrome, Firefox, and Edge browsers[1] and Naren is always prepared to start testing with WAVE when any web components are built part of their agile projects. The reason of picking WAVE rather than other tools is very simple—it is available as a plugin, and he approaches his developer Mark to get this extension installed on Mark's Chrome browser to allow scanning the small components when built and quickly analyze the defects and issues to fix during the Unit Testing Phase itself. That is a clever way to prevent defects rather than discovering them in later stages. But it does not mean that Naren needs to skip all his manual accessibility tests. He will still start to work on his accessibility tests since WAVE is just the beginning of accessibility implementation.

After clicking on "Add Extension" from the source of the WAVE plugin, Wave Evaluation Tool gets added to respective browser and clicking on the extension on the browser when your target website is opened, will let the WAVE tool quickly scan the website to provide a list of accessibility evaluation under five sections:

- Summary
- Details
- Reference
- Structure
- Contrast

In addition, an option is provided to switch Styles OFF or ON. This is to simulate the behavior of how users with partial vision loss, use the websites to avoid displaying complex styles, such as animation, fast moving styles by keeping them OFF.

Navigation:
After launching the target website to verify accessibility guidelines, clicking on the WAVE browser extension will open a section to the left hand side of the browser with evaluation report as below:

DOI: 10.1201/9781003299431-5

Picture: OrangeHRM[2]- An open source website tested against accessibility guidelines using WAVE tool.

When WAVE provided a basic evaluation report, it is easy to click on each item marked on the website to understand the evaluation and accessibility reference to it. Alternatively, it is possible to click on "View Details" at the left hand side menu to display complete issues, which is opened in "Details" section:

Even though the list of accessibility errors, alerts, and features are provided, they may not be clear on why they are getting listed and what guidelines are related to it. So, there is a nice feature in each issue with two links, such as Reference and Code. While clicking on different parts of the alert, the website itself will open a small dialog box of WAVE, which provides those two links in which clicking on Reference will display right accessibility guidelines reference in left hand side and clicking on code will display the DOM elements in which the error has been identified.

Even though WAVE provides a detailed report on accessibility evaluation, it still may not be 100% of everything we are looking for the website to adhere to. Hence, testing using screen readers and assistive technologies like zoom text are essential and important to complete full round of manual tests to prove that the website is adhered to guidelines and accessible to users. After performing defect fixes post manual tests, those added attributes such as "alt-text" can be updated part of automated tests, such as selenium automated tests to run as Accessibility Regression Suite.

Responsibilities of Front-End Engineers and Shift Left Testing

Performing WAVE-based evaluation during the web development by front-end engineers is very important and most recommended during the application development life cycle. Alternatively,

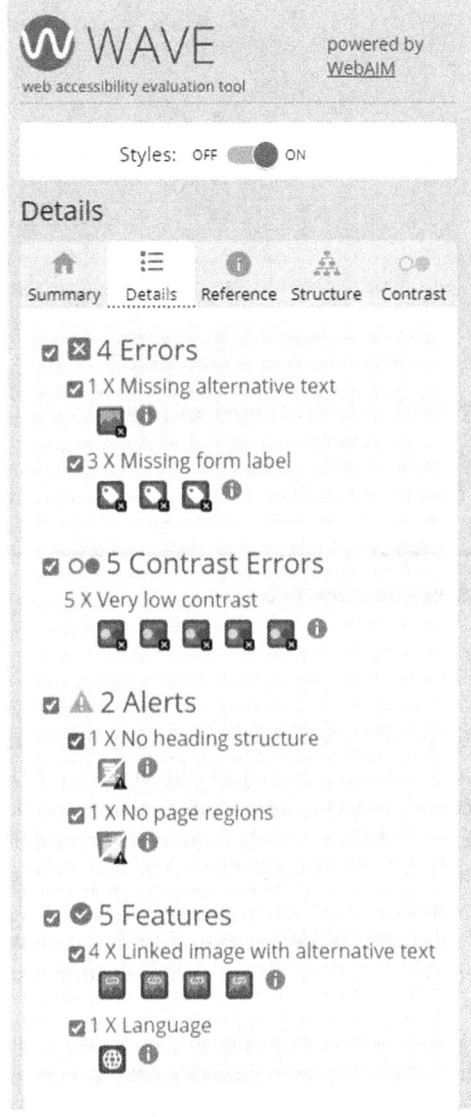

Picture: WAVE displays list of errors and issues from the sample website.

quality engineers can perform WAVE evaluation when front-end engineers build a fresh web page that is merged to their code base.

If code gets merged to target branch, getting WAVE evaluation needs a set of defect fixes further. Hence, careful consideration of a shift left testing practice by performing WAVE evaluation before code merge will help prevent the defects rather than leaking to next stages of testing.

Picture: WAVE report of issues and references.

Alternatives

AxeDevTools[3] from deque is one of the best extensions available as an alternative to WAVE and it has AxeGuidedTests that is user friendly and easy to scan and identify first hand defects from any websites. This has been discussed in detail along with selenium automation tool implementation in my book earlier with the title "Advanced Selenium Web Accessibility Testing."[4]

Axe Guided Tests are really helpful to formulate the strategy around website scanning to get the meaning accessibility evaluation.

Note that while writing this book, WAVE version 3.1.6 has been used and requesting readers to use the latest version whenever available to make use of such opportunity to scan the website to get the list of accessibility issues.

So far, we learnt about WAVE and AxeDevTools. Let us directly get into the first set of web accessibility tests on few critical html elements in next chapter. If you are thinking to start your first set of tests in web accessibility, page title is a good place to explore defects.

Notes

1. Title: WAVE Browser Extensions. (Accessed 12 December 2021). Retrieved from https://wave.webaim.org/extension/
2. Title: OrangeHRM Open Source Application-Free to use under the GNU General Public License. (Accessed 12 December 2021). Retrieved from https://github.com/orangehrm/orangehrm
3. Title: axe DevTools - Web Accessibility Testing. (Accessed 12 December 2021). Retrieved from https://chrome.google.com/webstore/detail/axe-devtools-web-accessib/lhdoppojpmngadmnindnejefpokejbdd
4. Title: Advanced Selenium Web Accessibility Testing: Software Automation Testing Secrets Revealed. (Accessed 12 December 2021). Retrieved from https://www.momentumpress.net/books/advanced-selenium-web-accessibility-testing-software-automation-testing-secrets-revealed

Chapter 5

Website Page Title-based Accessibility Development

Accessibility Four Tests

As we know, users with disability use screen readers or assistive technologies to access web pages from computer devices, such as laptops. Hence it is appropriate to run the screen reader-based tests on each application change when deployed for testing cycle.

Our UAT Accessibility Tester and regular user of the website, Mr. CBK, knows this and he run these four tests in all the releases—no matter if the changes are affecting these four areas or not. On the contrary, it is not the case with functional tester Naren, since he can't run all the 200+ accessibility manual tests within 3 days of integration tests cycle, hence he just handpicked subset of tests from complete regression tests and performed manual accessibility checks using screen readers. You will see the defects he misses by following this approach in the next section.

When Naren asked on CBK's vision loss and the problems around it, CBK said a nice quote:

> **"Vision loss doesn't means vision less; Anyone can be a virtual visionary and having eyes or ears are not mandatory to be a super human; All you need is a little happiness every day to start the day".**

Page Title Tests

Users with disability practise to live with their difficulties and use screen readers for the site usages through their computers and features, such as voice over/talk back on mobile devices. If a normal user tries to book their COVID-19 vaccination through online website, it takes few minutes to launch the website. However, this is not same with users with disabilities, such as people with neural disorders (as an example). Those special users launch screen readers such as JAWS or NVDA before launching the websites. When the screen reader starts announcing the interaction of keyboard actions, they start launching the website through browsers that are suitable with respective screen readers. For example, Google Chrome and Firefox are most used browsers along with NVDA screen reader where as Internet Explorer and Google Chrome are most used browsers along with JAWS screen reader as per the recent survey results[2].

When a website is launched with the help of screen reader, the first topic users (with disability) will be interested is none other than the page title. This is common for users with vision impairment and Mr. CBK usually raised this as a first accessibility defect during his UAT phases before using the website in real time. This may not be a problem for users such as Valar and Sandy since they both are not relying on screen readers to read the sites. But it is a primary issue for users such as Guna and CBK since they can't have 100% visual experience like normal users. Whereas this is not same with normal users since most of the normal users try to get familiarize with content and feature to perform necessary actions on what are interested to proceed with the site soon after loading the content. This is also the same reason why most of the testers forget to check the meaning and relevance of page title from HTML elements while testing the target web pages.

Let us analyze this small piece of HTML code and see what challenges or what defects are detected in the page title section?

```
<!DOCTYPE html>
<html>
<head>
  <title>Booking your flight tickets</title>
</head>
<body>
<h1>Booking your flight tickets</h1>
<p>This is a paragraph within the web page.</p>
</body>
</html>
```

When a tester reads this page title part of accessibility testing, it would easy be updated as "PASS." But let us understand on what will happen when users with disability are listening to this page title.

They would ask following questions in most of the times:

- Screen reader announces the web page as "Booking your flight tickets"—Does it mean a fake website, as no brand or company details were mentioned?
- How about amending flight tickets or checking flight schedule?—This website title did not announce anything about it.

Henceforth, this title is a valid defect to raise against WCAG standards; still many testers argue that the page title is presented hence it is not a defect. But it is a defect just because the title is not meaningful.

What will a Good Defect Look Like?

Subject: As per WCAG 2.4.2 page title is not meaningful and does not contain the company name, purpose, and features.

Description: Page tile is vague with no clarity on brand, page details, and what is expected when users visited the web page.

Type of the Defect: Valid Defect

Severity: 2

What will a Poorly Articulated Defect Looks Like?

Subject: Page title is incorrect

Description: Page tile needs a change as it is not useful

Type of the Defect: Suggestion

Severity: 4

What will a Better Fix to this Defect?

After receiving defect description, front-end developer M updated the title in the HTML page as below:

```
<!DOCTYPE html>
<html>
<head>
  <title>Official Skyflightjet website to book international flights</title>
</head>
<body>
<h1>Booking your flight tickets</h1>
<p>This is a paragraph within the web page.</p>
</body>
</html>
```

After getting this title update, Mark was interested to push the code immediately to live environments to get the fix deployment soon, hence he made the defect status from "InProgress" to "'Ready to Release." But our tester N stopped that approach for a valid reason and switched the status to "InProgress."

Shift Left Testing on Page Title

When Mark interested the fix to go live without testing, our QE, N wanted a shift left testing to be performed on Mark's laptop itself. This made Mark to think that N is making the simple fix too complicated. But N bought time from Mark to show what he wanted to do. He first installed

NVDA screen reader in Mark's Windows laptop and launched the code fix in localhost (through local branch) and started listening to screen reader.

That is the first moment when Mark understood that the launching of this particular website reading the page title as *Official Skyflightjet Website to Book International Flights*. Now that the fix is tested in Mark's local code and he was assuming that the code will directly get a green signal to push to master. But N was not ready yet.

Redeployment of the code in test environment for an Integration Testing

N deployed the code fix along with several other fixes made for an upcoming major release and he found the html of the page changed as below:

```
<!DOCTYPE html>
<html>
<head>
</head>
<body>
<h1>This is a heading of the web page</h1>
<p>This is a paragraph within the web page.</p>
</body>
</html>
```

After seeing the title section getting missed, N reopened the defect with status "ReOpen" and assigned it back to Mark.

As a surprise they both found an another defect fix forcefully removing entire title components of the site pages and it thus caused the issue.

Now Mark worked with his development peers and letting N to test the code once again in integration test environment.

Latest code after redeployment:

```
<!DOCTYPE html>
<html>
<head>
  <title></title>
</head>
<body>
<h1>This is a heading of the web page</h1>
<p>This is a paragraph within the web page.</p>
</body>
</html>
```

Our tester, N has not made the test to PASS yet since the title section is available but it is empty for one of the subpages.

Mark once again took the defect back to his development team and got the issues resolved to display title in all the main pages and sub pages of the website and N tested it until complete integration testing and sent it to CBK for UAT phase.

Now coming back to CBK on his UAT tests, he passed the defect for immediate release, which was a good news. But after 4-months time, during a UAT regression testing of recent release, he made the defect to move from "LIVE" to "Re-Open" once again. Mark initially thought it was a mistake but later realized that something went wrong in the live code and wanted to know why this defect is reopened once again?

While speaking to CBK, it was realized that launching this website is no longer announcing any page title details through screen readers.

Now there is a question put forward to N, our tester who uses screen reader in test environments before releasing to live on every releases:

Why Did You Miss Running this Test using Screen Reader in Test Environments When the Page Title was Missing from HTML?

Mr. N mentioned that he only handpicked subsets of manual accessibility tests for every release as a regression test since most of them are manual and it is not ideal to automate screen readers.

Moral of the story: even though N tests the website with subset of manual accessibility tests, it is not possible for him to verify accessibility in every build manually—this has to be automated wherever possible. It is not possible to automate the interactions of screen readers due to current limitations in the toolsets. But it is possible to automate the html properties of the website in which the screen readers picking up the content to read to users. In this section, we discuss about page title and this content sourced from <title> section of the html page by screen readers, hence verifying title property through an automated test will help in verifying the accessibility-related properties in every build, hence if the title section was missed in future builds, it will be easy to identify through systematic-scheduled CI/CD tests.

How to Write an Automated Test to Verify Such Defect Fix Part of Accessibility Automation Regression Test?

CypressIO-based JavaScript is easy to write and run on the web pages to verify the page title to match with the expected text of the site.

Assuming that we are testing the page title of an open source demo HR website to write a regression test on accessibility and business analysts is okay with the title provided on the site (assumption).

Update a function that checks the title xpath through assertion should command that check the existence of such page title on the site.

```
const pageTitle_Home = '//*[@title=\'OrangeHRM\']'

export const loginOrangehrmPage = {
  verifyPageTitle () {
```

```
   cy.xpath(pageTitle_Home)
        .should('exist')
   }
}
```

Once function is written, call it from a step definition:

```
Then('the page title should exist on home page', () => {
   loginOrangehrmPage.verifyPageTitle()
})
```

Next step is to write a small feature file to test this defect fix:

```
Feature: Verify the Page Title from Home Page of OrangeHRM Website to adhere to WCAG
Success Criterian 2.4.2

    Scenario: WCAG SC242 Test on Page Title
        Given I open OrangeHRM homepage
        When I SignIn as user
        Then the page title should exist on home page
```

In addition to all these steps, it is always advisable to record the video of the tests to review the results with team whenever possible. Hence, this can be made possible by adding two lines in cypress.json file:

```
{
"video":true
}
```

This is a sample website identified to test the page title through cypress automated tests and it can be verified in GitHub open source framework in the pull request here:

https://github.com/narayananpalani/cypress-test-techniques/pull/16

Command to run this test in Google Chrome:

```
npx cypress run--spec cypress\integration\features\wcag242PageTitleTest.feature--browser
chrome
```

Screenshot:

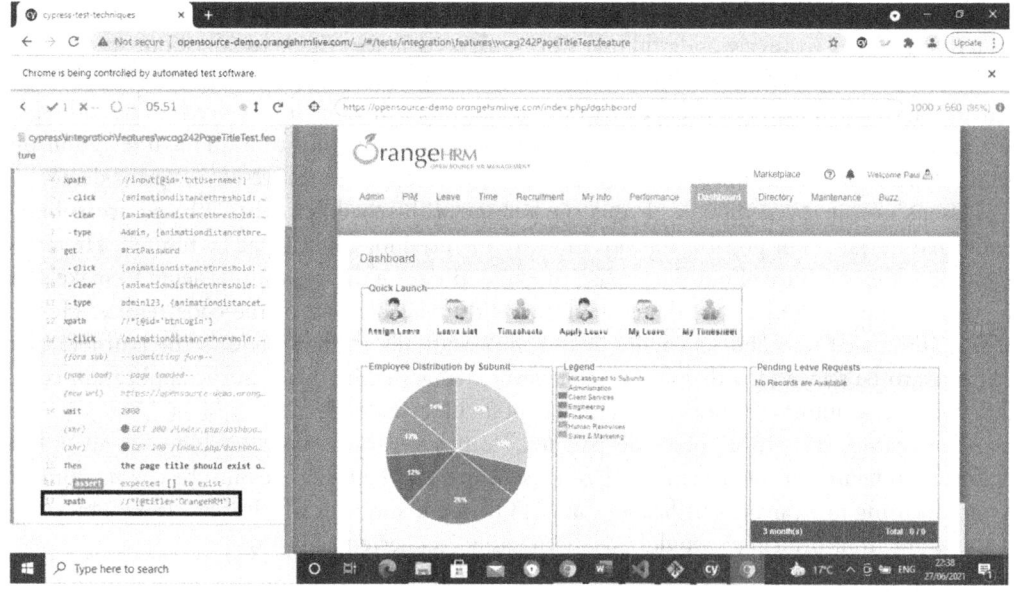

Picture: Image of the cypress automated tests that control the chrome browser to interact with website.

Writing Automated Tests is an End of Story—Is it Really True?

After 10 months of time of first release, during a UAT regression testing, CBK made the defect to move from "LIVE" to "Re-Open" once again. Mark has been extremely unhappy about this defect at the last minute and asked the reason on why this defect is reopened once again?

While speaking to CBK, it was realized that the recent architectural changes made the website to move toward a single page application (instead having multiple subpages) to book both international and domestic flights in AJAX web page. But this is not reflecting on the title and the title is still holding the same content as before (as *Official Skyflightjet website to book international flights*).

Now there is a million dollar question to N, our favorite functional tester who also runs integration testing in test environments:

Why Did You Miss Running this Test in Test Environments When the Page Design Changed to Single Page Application?

Mr. N started talking after a brief silence with his murmuring voice "page title was not transparently visible from website hence I could not differentiate when the design is changed through manual tests. Moreover, this page title accessibility tests are automated and running in CI/CD tests and it is passing all the time, hence it was missed from user requirement and not from testing department."

Why did a BA Missed to Include this Page Title Checks in Her Acceptance Criteria?

Even though Juliet writes a wonderful user story with acceptance criteria to talk about accessibility guidelines, it was not her mandate to cover the requirement to update page title when page structure and design has been changed part of the user story. It is by default needs to be addressed as a regular periodic "accessibility automated test-result review" in a continuous integration pipeline to make sure that functional testers discuss the title-related test result in sprint demo.

Lessons Learnt: Even though N tests the website with scheduled CI/CD-based accessibility automated test, it is not possible for him to verify the need for title change by himself. He needs to question the relevance of out-dated page title to entire team during a sprint demo to make sure the entire team is happy about the current page title available part of the code release. Hence, writing automated tests and scheduling it to run periodically is not an end to the journey. Test results are to be reviewed with full team whenever changes taking place in the application code. Otherwise these automated tests are simply a "pesticide paradox."

After hearing this word "pesticide paradox," our tester N is now searching for an online dictionary to figure out the true meaning of these words and I am sure he must be cursing himself for not focusing to clear the certification on ISTQB foundations in which if he cleared, meaning of this word from principle5 would have been easily recollected as below:

> *"If the same tests are repeated over and over again, eventually the same set of test cases will no longer find any new defects. To overcome this "pesticide paradox", test cases need to be regularly reviewed and revised, and new and different tests need to be written to exercise different parts of the software or system to find potentially more defects."*
>
> Source: http://istqbfoundation.wikidot.com/printer--friendly//1#toc16

Credits to @ISTQB board for documenting this wonderful principle part of the syllabus. Now N is not only thinking to study for foundation exam but he rewrote his automated test to remove the error in his test code as below:

```
const pageTitle_Home = '//*[@title=\'Skyflightjet website to book domestic and international flights \']'

export const skyFlightJetPageTitleCheck = {
  verifyPageTitle () {
    cy.xpath(pageTitle_Home)
      .should('exist')
  }
}
```

He is only worried about exam fees reimbursement from his manager and as a reader, you would have guessed it right that he may not get the money reimbursed if he got failed attempts as co-incidentally he failed the test twice already and does not want to fail one more time.

Advanced Page Title Testing

After seeing the defect retest history of page title related code, Engineering Lead knows that the release is not going according to the plan. "Okay. I want an external consultant to test the code before next major release." After getting Claire's direction (Engineering Lead), the team is now waiting to involve Nick, external consultant (100% visually impaired) to test the web pages. After hearing the history of the defects in small piece of page title code and testing the same pages for few minutes, Nick replies in a exasperated voice, "What kind of bullshit code is this?"

"I go for launching each page in separate tabs of the browser and each page is reading in this format from screen reader:

Page1: <title>**Official Skyflightjet website to book international flights**</title>
Page2: <title>**Skyflightjet website:Amend or Cancel flights**</title>
Page3: <title>**Skyflightjet website:book domestic flights**</title>
Page4: <title>**Skyflightjet website:Help and Support**</title>
Page5: <title>**Skyflightjet website:Contact Us**</title>
Page6: <title>**Skyflightjet website:FAQs**</title>

So it took almost few seconds for me to wait to figure out which page is for what purpose if I am navigating between the tabs using keyboard shortcut Ctrl+Tab which is not right. It has to be other way around. You should have written the purpose first and the brand next. In addition to that the heading level one and title should explain same context since both are meant to read same objective and scope for the website visitors"

After the key recommendations received from external consultant, Mark, the front-end developer made key changes to complete page lists as below:

Page1: <title>**Book international flights: Skyflightjet website**</title>
Page2: <title>**Amend or Cancel flights: Skyflightjet website**</title>
Page3: <title>**Book domestic flights: Skyflightjet website**</title>
Page4: <title>**Help and Support: Skyflightjet website**</title>
Page5: <title>**Contact Us: Skyflightjet website**</title>
Page6: <title>**Frequently Asked Questions: Skyflightjet website**</title>

In addition to changes above, he made the changes to heading as below:

```
<!DOCTYPE html>
<html>
<head>
  <title>Book international flights: Skyflightjet website</title>
</head>
<body>
<h1>Book international flights: Skyflightjet website</h1>
```

```
<p>This is a paragraph within the web page.</p>
</body>
</html>
```

Lessons Learnt: Your team may run advanced test automation in a scheduled DevOps pipeline but it needs an expert eye to spot that magical defect hiding inside the code somewhere in the corners. That expenditure to bring an external accessibility consultant is a best investment to make your special customers (with disabilities) satisfied all the time.

Finally, a quote from CBK on page title: "**Every website is like a virtual home and 'page title' is your doorstep; When the page title is missing from website, it means that the user with disability will never get a chance to enter into the home without someone's help; If you build an expensive home, you need to think on accessible walk way too as you may get a guest anytime with a wheel chair to come in; Similarly, if you are building an expensive website, you need an accessible and meaning page title to understand on what it is built for**"

We learnt about page title-based accessibility tests in this chapter but it is not everything in web accessibility yet. Language is one of the critical tests to conduct in websites to prove that they function appropriately when different set of users from different language background interact with the website. Naren starts with page title tests first but he quickly moves on to language-based verifications since he always knew that many organizations missed to check this fundamental aspect while releasing their websites for target users.

Notes

1. "ICICI Lombard | 20 Years Journey" YouTube video, (duration in 00:02:33) Posted by "ICICI Lombard" (Oct 7, 2019), video source: https://www.youtube.com/watch?v=qjgmV-mYJUU
2. Title: Screen Reader User Survey #8 Results. (Accessed 12 December 2021). Retrieved from https://webaim.org/projects/screenreadersurvey8/

Chapter 6

Website Language-based Accessibility Development

Web Page Language Tests

After launching screen readers, website is opened from a browser and the screen reader searches for DOM HTML semantic elements of the page to start reading about what the page is made for.

```
<html lang="en">
</html>
```

Language marked inside html tag is the first hint for screen reader to read the entire website in the English language. This is not same with websites of different languages.

Types of Users

- Users with disabilities who know only one language
- Users with disabilities who know multiple languages

Language Selection in NVDA Screen Reader

Most of the single language users have an option to choose a default language in screen reader, such as the option below as an example:

Install NVDA screen reader[2] and choose "Install NVDA in this computer" option after clicking on the installer.

It is also recommended to read user guide[3] of NVDA to use eSpeaker NG to choose one in 80 different languages they support for visually impaired users.

DOI: 10.1201/9781003299431-7

Preferences > Settings > Speech > Synthesizer-Click Change Button > Select eSpeak NG in the dropdown and click OK > In Voice dropdown, choose the language of your choice:

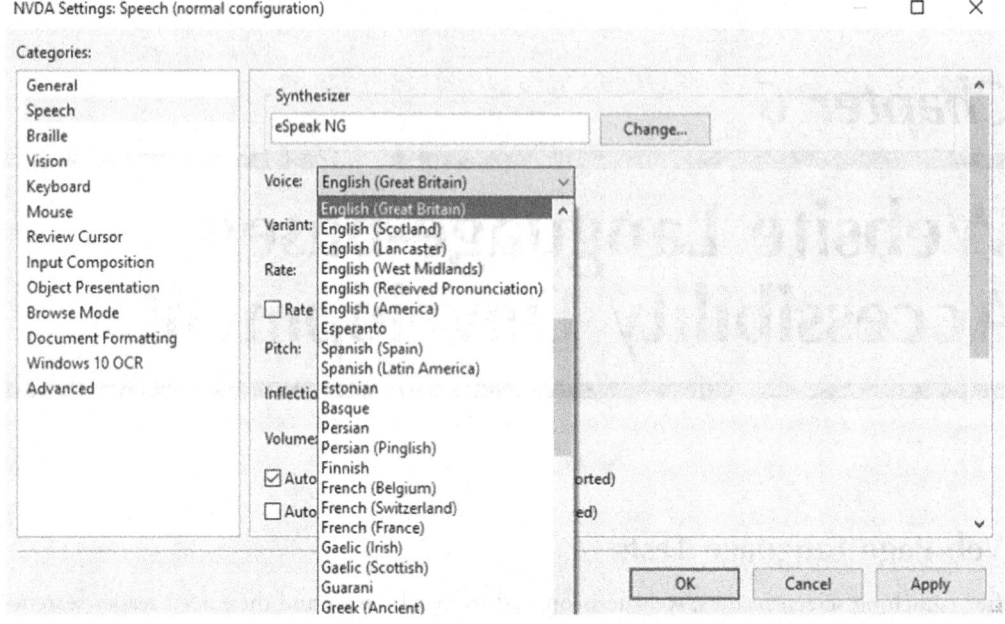

Picture: NVDA settings speech from NVDA screen reader.

Just 4.83% of the world population speaks English language as the native language (527 million) as per Washington post,[4] hence there are users with disabilities that use language of their choice in screen readers this way.

When user choses a default language in screen reader, it reads every website in the slang of the language being chosen. If user has chosen French as default language in eSpeakNG through NVDA, it reads every page (including English pages) in French mode/accent, hence it is confusing for users if lang attribute is missing from the webpage.

What is the Challenge if Lang Attribute is Missing from the Website?

If the web page is provided with lang attribute as described below, it will be easy for the screen reader to understand that the primary language of the website is English:

```
<html lang="en">
```

Hence, it reads the site in English accent.

On a different note, user choose Arabic as their default language in screen reader (as an example) and the site missing the lang attribute but written in English results in the screen reader voice reading the site in Arabic accent, hence user will not be in a position to understand anything from the content.

What will a Good Defect Look Like?

Subject: As per WCAG 3.1.1 language of the page is missing from html attributes

Description: When lang attribute is missing from html of the web page as lang="en", it is read by screen reader using the accent of the default language pre-set by users with disabilities hence it creates difficulty in understanding.

Type of the Defect: Valid Defect

Severity: 2

What will a Poorly Articulated or Incorrect Defect Look Like?

Subject: Language attribute missing from html, hence it is requested to announce the language of the page in page title

Description: Page title can be used to let user know that the page written in English language since lang attribute is missing

Type of the Defect: Suggestion

Severity: 4

Reason: Page title can not be the replacement for lang attribute since page title itself announced in the accent of default language chosen in screen reader hence user may not get it interpreted correctly in first few instances.

Lessons Learnt: Incorrect lang attribute such as lang= "English" or completely missing this lang attribute in html elements results in incorrect pronunciation rules, incorrect accent, and extreme difficulty in understanding the meaning when screen reader has been setup with default language of non-english type.

Language Preferences on Part of the Content within Websites

Now there is a new requirement to add a paragraph for French users in English website as below:

Passengers arriving at paris needs to fill in formulaire d'arrivée

This is a new requirement for Naren in addition to test the section of website (English based) to check few words in French. Hence, Naren who speaks both English and French installed NVDA with English (Britain) as default language and tried to test the code which has below elements:

```
<p> Passengers arriving at paris needs to fill in formulaire d'arrivée
</p>
```

After testing this sentence, he found that the French word was also spoken with English pronunciation (instead of French pronunciation).

He went on to raise a defect and assign it to Mark.

Subject: As per WCAG 3.1.1 language of the word is pronounced incorrect (using English pronunciation)

Description: Since the lang attribute is marked as "en" in html, the word "formulaire d'arrivée" has been pronounced with English accent and it has to be read by screen reader in French accent.

Type of the Defect: Valid Defect

Severity: 2

After seeing this defect, Mark has come forward to appreciate Naren on his excellent work by finding this interesting defect. Even though the html lang has been marked as "en," Mark went on to update the paragraph as below:

```
<p>Passengers arriving at paris needs to fill in "<span lang="fr"> formulaire d'arrivée
</span>".
```

Now Naren retested the defect and found the right pronunciation while attempting to read the French word.

Lessons Learnt: Please search for the complete webpage on the content provided in different languages or signs to make sure that they are pronounced right for the customers on their language preferences.

Write automated tests using CypressIO on Language Verification

After verifying the language once, it is highly recommended to write a small xpath object to verify it in automated tests as below:

```
const loginPageLang = '//*[@lang=\'en\']'

verifyPageLanguage () {
  cy.xpath(loginPageLang)
      .should('exist')
}
```

Once these functions are written, it can be used in a step definition as below:

```
Then('the language of the page should exist on login page', () => {
  loginOrangehrmPage.verifyPageLanguage()
})
```

Next step is to write a simple feature file to verify this language attribute:

Feature: Verify the Language of OrangeHRM Website to adhere to WCAG Success Criterian 3.1.1 by having lang attribute as english

Scenario: WCAG SC311 Test on Page Title
Given I open OrangeHRM homepage
Then the language of the page should exist on login page

In this section, we learnt about how Naren tested language of websites using different settings in NVDA and automating after manual checks through Cypress and learnt about few test automation scripts as well. But Naren has plenteous of manual accessibility tests pending to prove that the website is truly adhering to all the accessibility guidelines. His next preference is to explore through landmarks of websites. Landmarks may be one of the feature for normal users but it is a critical feature for users with disabilities since they find it hard to read everything in a website through screen reader, hence they try to interact with website through landmarks and these landmarks are thus needed to be verified before releasing to customers.

Notes

1. "Loving Akhilesh - Reflections of Parenting a Child with Severe Learning Disabilities" YouTube video, [duration in 00:55:00] Posted by "Srilekhini Kadari" (Aug 24, 2021), video source: https://www.youtube.com/watch?v=RCwQLWWV9cM
2. Title: Download and experience NVDA today. (Accessed 12 December 2021). Retrieved from https://www.nvaccess.org/download/
3. Title: NVDA Configuration Profiles. (Accessed 12 December 2021). Retrieved from https://www.nvaccess.org/files/nvda/documentation/userGuide.html#ConfigurationProfiles
4. Title: The world's languages, in 7 maps and charts. (Accessed 12 December 2021). Retrieved from https://www.washingtonpost.com/news/worldviews/wp/2015/04/23/the-worlds-languages-in-7-maps-and-charts/

Chapter 7

Website Landmarks-based Accessibility Development

Even our Engineering Lead C herself uses screen reader since she suffers from memory loss and wanted to register the voices while going through the web application journey, so that she doesn't miss it due to short-term memory. It is more common in users with visual impairment and CBK uses the screen reader along with zoom-assist technologies, such as ZoomText or Windows Magnifier, all the time.

He once told Naren that he likes more of NVDA (Non Visual Desktop Access) Screen Reader when comparing to other screen readers since he is unable to afford the license fee for the licensed screen readers, where as NVDA is made 100% open source,thanks to NVDA founders Michael Curran and James Teh, for making it a free screen reader to provide benefits to everyone in need and not having enough money to support the screen reader license costs.

Discussions with CBK during coffee time is always fun, since he knows where the coffee vending machine is and what buttons to operate without even seeing anything on the office floor most of the times. Recently, he mentioned about irregularities of many screen readers in picking up words from HTML5 and WAI-ARIA roles.

He was mentioning the roles:

https://developer.mozilla.org/en-US/docs/Web/Accessibility/ARIA/Roles

When Naren asked to explain little details, CBK opens the websites through browser, and pressed INSERT+F7 as a first step to see "Listed Links" from the entire page, hence he can choose where to go from the page when it is launched.

This is not the same behavior with normal users since most of the users try to launch the web page and read it out to decide on where to click. Whereas users with disabilities may not or need not use mouse and they rely on keyboard most of the times to navigate using keyboard shortcuts.

Especially pressing "INSERT+F7" when screen reader and browser launched result in displaying five options through radio buttons:

- Links
- Headings

DOI: 10.1201/9781003299431-8

- Form Fields
- Buttons
- Landmarks

So he managed to navigate to right landmark based on the options available. But it is not as simple as it seems.. It is the main area where loads of accessibility-related defects are unattended in popular websites.

Listed Links

Let us see a couple of images from one of the popular websites on Elements List. CBK pressed "INSERT+F7" and he heared the linked lists in first instance from NVDA:

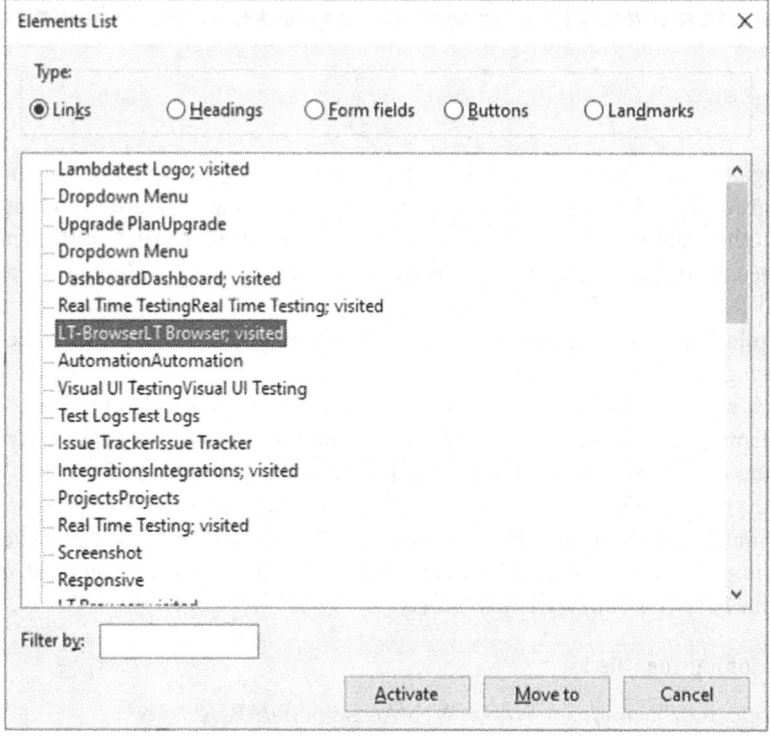

Picture: Image of NVDA elements list displaying links of a website.

Elements list is picked up from "href" attributes in the entire html semantic elements. It is worth to make a note on "Name," "Role," and "Value" of each link to represent detailed information on the linked list, hence a user can decide which link to choose according to their needs.

Headings List

Heading List

After pressing "INSERT+F7" (when NVDA is launched along with browser), selecting Headings radio button will make display available H1, H2, H3 of the website:

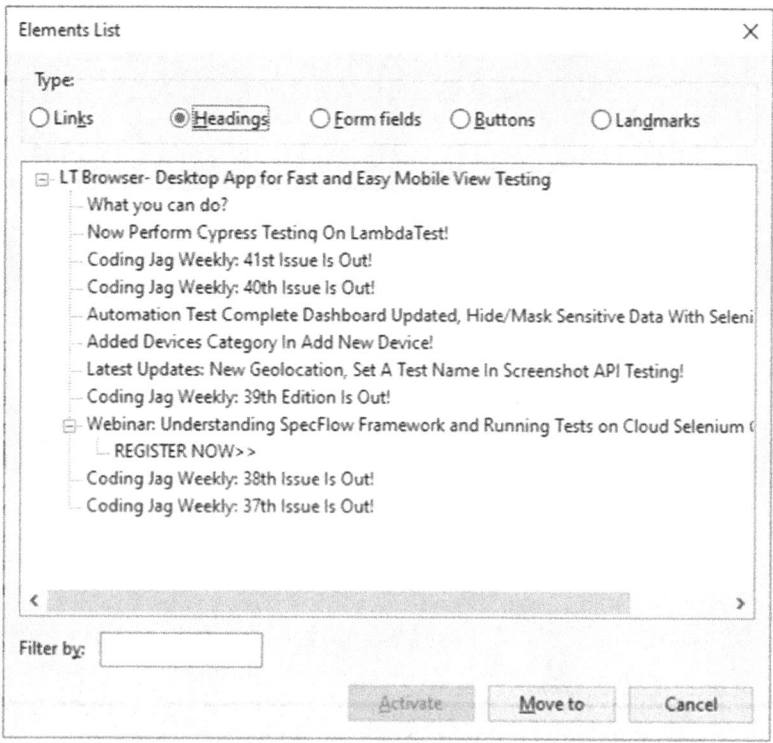

Picture: Image of NVDA elements list displaying headings of a website.

This is where testers are to be very careful to read out to understand the hierarchy of the headings structure. If H3 available without H1 and H2, it is a defect since there is no clear hierarchy for the page elements.

Form Fields

Each input fields such as user name and password are listed down part of form fields, hence users can select the right field to navigate immediately by Activate button:

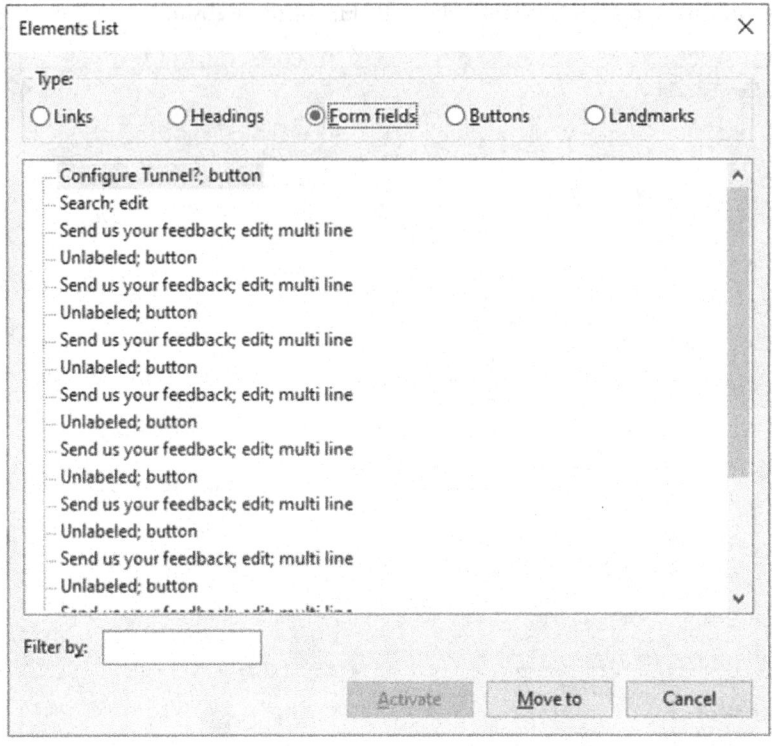

Picture: Image of NVDA elements list displaying form fields of a website.

Buttons

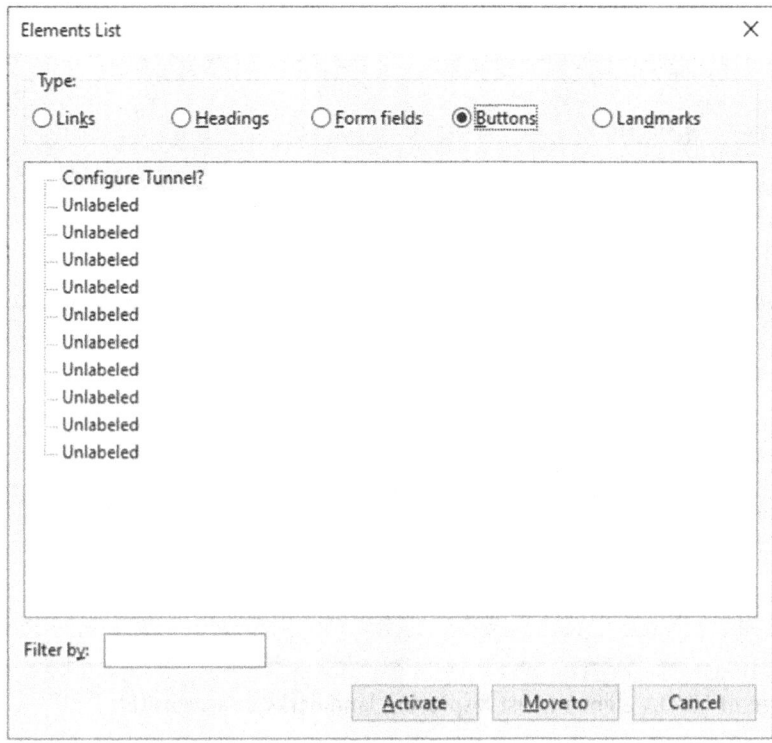

Picture: Image of NVDA elements list displaying buttons of a website.

Landmarks

Those HTML sections marked as role="form" have been announced by majority of the screen readers in Landmarks section:

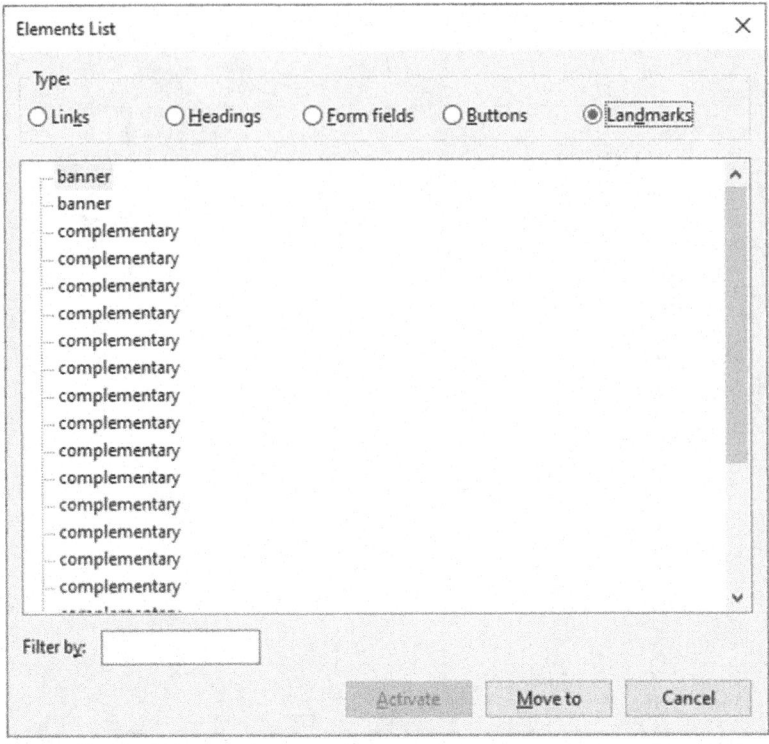

Picture: Image of NVDA elements list displaying landmarks of a website.

In the screenshot provided (related to landmarks), it is clearly evident that "complementary" is not a right representation of any landmarks on a website, hence users with visual impairment can't differentiate between them.

In the next four days since speaking to CBK, Naren has been thinking about "Linked Lists" endlessly. There are three items that are a bit complicated to test—they are forms, regions, and articles.

Screen Readers Announcing Form Elements

HTML5 format: <form>
ARIA format: role="form"

Some screen readers support reading the native html5 element as long as <form> is mentioned in the web application. But some needed a dedicated ARIA as role="form" to recognize the section to announce in landmark section. This is extremely complex for Naren since he does not have time to test in all major screen readers to test this one element to check where it is not been announced clearly. Hence, he is now thinking to recommend front-end engineer Mark to add ARIA as role="form" wherever appropriate.

As a test and learn, Naren picked an open source and found a form attribute that is not recognized in NVDA screen reader:

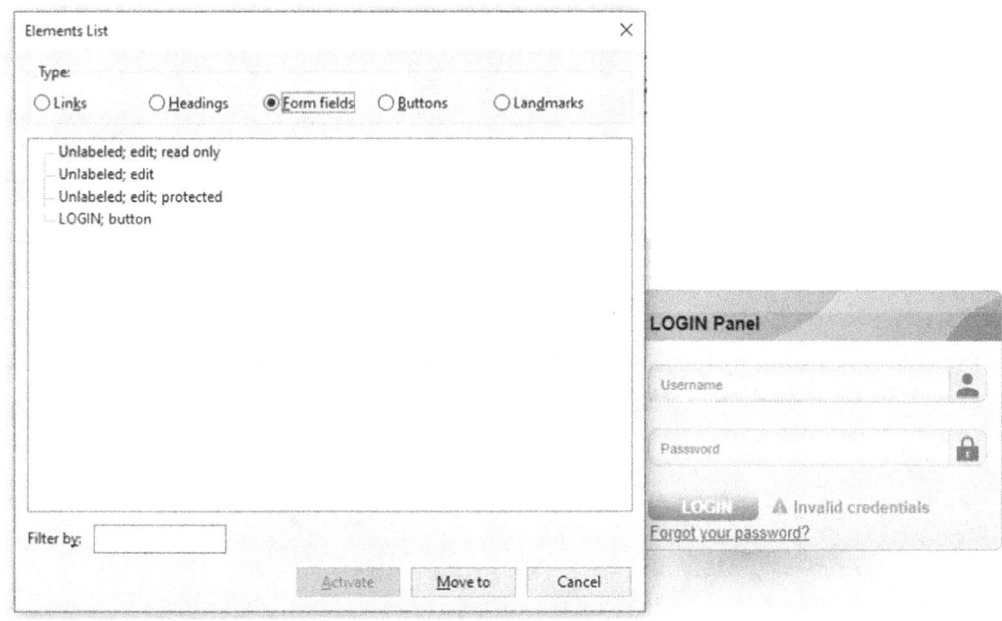

Picture: Image of NVDA elements list displaying form fields of a website which contains login user name, password along with login button and forgot your password? link.

In form fields, login user name and login password fields are read like "Unlabeled" hence it makes a 100% visually impaired candidate to think on what the fields really are? If Nicholas T, our accessibility testing consultant tests it, definitely it is going to be a SEVERIT 2 classified defect to get fixed.

At the same time, the same page-related landmarks are surprisingly empty:

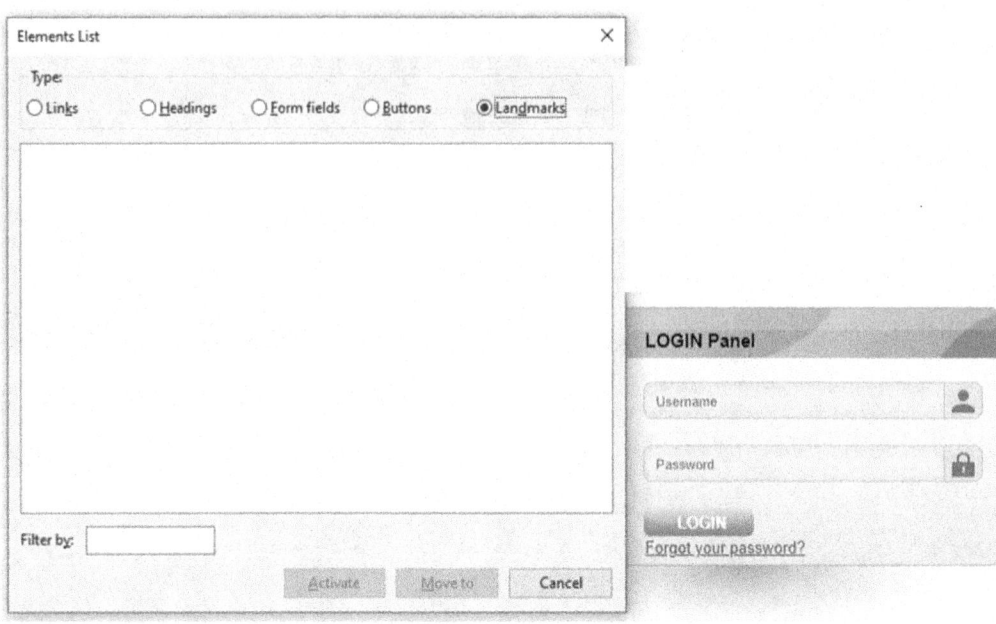

Picture: Image of NVDA elements list displaying empty landmarks of a website which contains login user name, password along with login button and forgot your password? link.

This is due to the reason that the form section is missing a role property:

```
<form id="frmLogin" method="post" action="/index.php/auth/validateCredentials">
</form>
```

Lessons Learnt: As a best practice, HTML native elements are highly recommended to use when possible. But cases like form need a dedicated role to be added to benefit users with majority of the screen readers with respect to 100% test coverage. Else users with disabilities won't be in a position to identify the landmark to navigate to form elements.

Summary

HTML elements are recognized by screen readers:

Tool	<title>	<header>	<footer>	<nav>	<main>	<section>	<article>	<form>	<aside>
NVDA	YES	YES	YES	YES	YES	Few Screen Readers support			YES
JAWS	YES	YES	YES	YES	YES				YES
Others	YES	YES	YES	YES	YES				YES

Recommended ARIA attributes for each HTML elements if screen readers are failing to read the items while navigating to each section:

HTML5 Element	ARIA Role Attribute
<header>	role="banner"
<main>	role="main"
<footer>	role="contentinfo"
<title>	role="banner"
<nav>	role="navigation"
<section>	role="region"
<article>	role="article"
<form>	role="form"
<aside>	role="complementary"

Reference:
https://developer.mozilla.org/en-US/docs/Web/Accessibility/ARIA/Roles/Navigation_Role

Now that our UAT specialist Mr. CBK asked an interesting question to Naren, QE, that what will happen if the same web application is launched in Internet Explorer 8 to check accessibility guidelines? To his surprise, the screen readers were reading correctly when he navigated through TAB key of the keyboard from top to bottom of the web page but some of the elements were skipped when navigating backward from bottom to top through SHIFT+TAB keyboard shortcut.

Thus he went back to CBK and he gave a wonderful suggestion:

Add display:block in CSS

There are three types of displays useful when considering the html5 elements to get rendered in old browsers, such as Internet Explorer 8. They are,

```
display:inline
display:inline-block
display:block
```

He suggested the front-end developer Mark to implement the CSS properties, such as this as an example:

```
span.c {
display: block;
}
```

But the question from Naren is that why we need CSS properties to be amended in addition to ARIA properties? As CBK says, "Old Browsers are not compatible when they are developed since latest JavaScript and HTML5 elements may not get reflected in the same way like latest version of the browsers. Hence adding CSS properties will help aligning the web elements."

What is display:block?
Paragraph, Headers, and other sections are been displayed as block with whitespace above and below (hence it won't allow any other html elements to go near to those blocks).

After Mark implemented display:block within the CSS properties, Naren tested the backward compatibility with the keyboard shortcut SHIFT+TAB while navigating on the website and as a solid fix, he could read most of the elements from screen reader.

As a next step Naren wanted to test the same behavior in JAWS screen reader and so he tried to open the listed links through keyboard shortcut INSERT+F7 but they weren't displayed. After few hours of frustration, he approached to CBK. With a smile on his face, he gave a table with keyboard shortcuts to Naren:

Screen Reader Name	Keyboard Shortcut to read landmarks
NVDA	INSERT+F7
JAWS	INSERT+F3
Mac Operating System-Safari Browser (After starting Voice Over)	Ctrl+Option+U, Once rotor has been opened use left/right arrows

We learnt about crucial landmark tests from Naren and how he used different keyboard shortcuts to interact with screen reader and website to find defects and to avoid such difficulties that real users with disabilities might face. Now he turned his attention to web page headings since headings are most crucial navigation elements for users to give correct location of topic for users to interact.

Chapter 8

Website Headings-based Accessibility Development

A few days ago, there was an organizational level All Hands Meet in which Claire requested their Chief Marketing Office Martin to speak about their grocery channel website and their overall popularity (in addition to flight business) in middle-east and the USA. By 11 A.M. in the morning, he started speaking in front of the entire engineering staffs:

> "we run a grocery store online and you may think that marketing department is the primary reason why our store is popular and selling well comparing to competitors. If you think in that way you are wrong. We have a catchy headings in each page of our website and Search Engine Optimisation (SEO) highlighting important parts of the website and getting the users to step into our virtual door through Google street. Hence this is primarily done through you engineers and I salute at your hard work and dedication in getting this website popular."

Hearing these words from CTO made Naren think differently about headings of the website. Despite the popularity, there are few visually impaired customers confused with some of the page headings and those calls to our telephone operators increased over the past few weeks. Hence Naren started searching the best way to test the headings of the websites as soon as possible.

The very first insight from Naren on the home page was that when customers search grocery items through search functionality, there are more search terminologies announced apart from headings (through screen reader) and nothing much on the links available, landmarks, form field details, etc. Since these meaningful structural information is missing these headings are not much useful to those customers with vision impairment.

What is read by screen reader at this stage?
"SFJ Grocery Search Results"

But he was not convinced with this heading announcement and he called Nicholas T over phone for a quick consultation.

DOI: 10.1201/9781003299431-9

"If you are announcing your heading through screen reader, make sure to include number of headings, links and landmarks available to get some insight around the overall page to those users with disabilities. So they know that they are dealing with a long page or short page and quickly get attention to right section to go to! It is something like a train announcement on how many stops are ahead hence the passenger can plan and prepare for the travel time."

This was a fruitful conversation Naren had and replied "Look, I know I have disturbed you in your busy schedule but what you told today is something precious and I am going to raise this as a defect to my team at the earlier."

When he launched his team's JIRA board, he raised a defect with classification as "Recommendation" and noted Nicholas' recommendation in the same defect.

Here it goes:

Subject: As per WCAG 2.4.6 page heading is not meaningful and does not contain the landmarks of the web page.

Description: Had a chat with Accessibility Consultant and he understood the test results and provided following insights:

> What is read by screen reader at this stage?
> "SFJ Grocery Search Results"
> What is supposed to be read by screen readers?
> "SFT Grocery Home Page with search results, three headings, five links, and eighteen landmarks"
> Note: It is recommended to maintain same title and heading text to announce through screen readers.

Type of the Defect: Recommendation

Severity: 2

Naren merely stepped in front of Mark's desk next day and asked about any defect fix updates and it was to his surprise that the defect were already fixed and available for retest in local test environment.

"Listen Naren, I love the way you find these defects when user story itself not clear on the accessibility guidelines. So better you test and tell me if it looks okay."

Forty-five minutes later, after Naren tested the page completely he was satisfied with the latest content of heading read as "SFT Grocery Home Page with search results, three headings, five links and eighteen landmarks." But the story is not over yet. Due to the increased texts on heading, it impacted the design of the page and few blocks were misaligned and Naren was not reopening the ticket to get it assigned to Mark again.

This time Mark added an aria-level attribute to avoid alignment issues and clarity on screen reader announcements:

```
<div role="heading" aria-level="1">
    SFT Grocery Home Page with search results, three headings, five links and eighteen
landmarks
</div>
```

Naren found it appropriate and closed the defect. As a accessibility tester, he learnt a key lesson thorugh this defect.

Lessons Learnt: Try adding aria-level for headings to avoid the misalignments or style breaking implementations when tested.

After the SIT phase, this was taken to CBK for UAT and he found a defect on landmarks, which grabbed a lot of attention from Mark again. This time the bug is not on alignment but on the content itself.

```
<h1>SFT Grocery Home Page with search results, three headings, five links and eighteen
landmarks</h1>
<h2>Section 1</h2>
<h2>Section 2</h2>
<h2>Section 3</h2>
   <h3>(i)</h3>
```

After hearing the announcements of these sections, CBK found them to be a bit generic and he recommended to get them with descriptive details in his bug description. After inviting CBK for a defect fix session, Mark and CBK together fixed the contents as below:

```
<h1>SFT Grocery Home Page with search results, three headings, five links and eighteen
landmarks</h1>
<h2>Favourites SFT Grocery</h2>
<h2>Find a Store SFT Grocery</h2>
<h2>Help SFT Grocery </h2>
   <h3>Contact Telephony SFT Grocery</h3>
```

Lessons Learnt: Landmarks such as heading 1, 2, 3 should be descriptive and informative for users with disabilities. It is recommended to include the need of descriptive heading texts within acceptance criteria of user stories.

In the four days since this application code went live, there were few announcements from the government to be incorporated in the grocery website in terms of COVID-19 pandemic guidelines and it was Mark, the front-end engineer, who made these announcements part of the header to make sure that the website adhered to the government guidelines.

```
<h1>SFT Grocery Home Page with search results, three headings, five links and eighteen
landmarks</h1>
<h1>Covid 19 Guidelines</h2>
<h3>Favourites SFT Grocery</h2>
<h3>Find a Store SFT Grocery</h2>
<h3>Help SFT Grocery</h2>
   <h3>Contact Telephony SFT Grocery</h3>
```

With the minimum functional testing (without a manual accessibility testing execution), this code underwent regression tests using automated tests in Jenkins pipeline and went into next stage. CBK raised at least two different defects in UAT phase.

Defect1: Suspecting the recent heading changes as a cause, CBK explains in the defect that heading level 2 is completely missing.

Defect2: Majority of the websites should have just one <h1>. This is to help understand where to find the beginning of the main content to navigate through keyboard shortcuts while using screen readers. But this code implementation has got two <h1>, which need review to fix.

Finally, Mark now agreed to fix both the defects in the following way:

```
<h1>SFT Grocery Home Page with search results, three headings, five links and eighteen
landmarks</h1>
<h2>Covid 19 Guidelines</h2>
<h2>Favourites SFT Grocery</h2>
<h2>Find a Store SFT Grocery</h2>
<h2>Help SFT Grocery</h2>
   <h3>Contact Telephony SFT Grocery</h3>
```

Lessons Learnt: Make sure that the hierarchical order has been maintained with proper sequence in headers. If there are any changes or any heading level skipped, try testing them through valid accessibility "manual" tests.

"I want you to remember the shortcuts table I gave you earlier" CBK asked Naren; recalling that table, Naren asked on how to navigate to headings specifically. But CBK told him to test and learn this time and he eventually found similar keyboard shortcuts for headings:

Screen Reader Name	Keyboard Shortcut to read headings
NVDA	INSERT+F7 opens element list and choose headings in radio buttons.
JAWS	INSERT+F6
Mac Operating System-Safari Browser (After starting Voice Over)	Ctrl+Option+U, Once rotor has been opened use left/right arrows to select headings

We learnt about several tips and tricks on testing headings in this section but we don't know yet on what are the tests where Naren really find useful defects in every software release. If a QA has to survive in industry, they should be capable enough to spot maximum defects. There is no doubt that "links" are the areas where many accessibility issues were found across the websites. Let us learn about how to test those links against accessibility guidelines in the next section. If a link does not adhere to accessibility standards, it will not only deviate users to difficulties but it may also create a deadlock situation for users with disabilities since broken links and unread, misread links create lot of confusion in user interactions.

Chapter 9

Website Links-based Accessibility Development

Despite developing the ReactJS pages with most advanced UI components, Mark got a question on how links work on websites when screen readers announce or try to click on them. He thought he needed advice from CBK on it and he enquired his suitable time to go through the list of links and respective href in his small web pages.

But unlike Naren, CBK recommended Mark to setup NVDA in his laptop and perform testing by sticking an A4 paper on the monitor and unplug mouse, in such way Mark cannot see what navigation he is going through. So CBK suggested him to navigate to links and try to perform click action without using mouse or cursor.

This has left Mark with trying all his keystrokes through keyboard to navigate to the grocery website and manage to navigate few links. But he was unable to move further to the entire page contents since there were more than hundred links in the entire code space.

Five hours later, Mark turned to CBK saying he doesn't know what to do in order to test all the links or glance on how many links are available overall in any web page. With a smile on his face, CBK mentioned that this is the way in which a 100% visiually impaired user struggles to navigate to any website if they are first timers with screen readers.

Lesson Learnt!
Now CBK shared a table with Mark to continue experiencing the links through screen reader, but this time using linked lists known as elements list:

Screen Reader Name	Keyboard Shortcut to read links
NVDA	INSERT+F7 to display elements list (or known as Linked Lists) in which select links radio button
JAWS	INSERT+F7
Mac Operating System-Safari Browser (After starting Voice Over)	Ctrl+Option+U, Once rotor has been opened use left/right arrows to move towards links

While learning the keyboard shortcuts, Mark learned that there is a test case written by Naren in the past:

DOI: 10.1201/9781003299431-10

Table: Test Case Sourced from GitHub Open Source on Web Accessibility Test Cases. [1]

		Target Application	https://opensource-demo.orangehrmlive.com/index.php/auth/validateCredentials
Role<s> Simulated in Test Case:			
Dependencies:		*OS Tested:*	
Test Information:		*Browser Tested:*	
Prepared by: Narayanan Palani		*Date:*	
Executed by:		*Time (hours):*	
Build Number:		*Level of Classification:*	A

*Subject	*Test Name	Description	Step Name	Step Description	Step Expected Results
Web_Accessibility	WCAG_2.4.4_LinkPurposeTests	This test case has been written to verify all functionality of the content is operable through a keyboard interface for verifying links using keyboard Refer to the WCAG Guidelines:https://www.w3.org/TR/UNDERSTANDING-WCAG20/visual-audio-contrast-text-presentation.html	Step 1	Launch NVDA Screen Reader from Windows Operating System and enable audio to listen to the screen reader Note: -Right click on NVDA, choose Tools and select Speech Viewer -Alternatively, Launch JAWS screen reader	Screen reader (NVDA or JAWS) should be launched successfully
			Step 2	Launch the browser and enter the URL of the website to test.	Website URL should be read out and display of the page should be read with title and other details.

Step 3	Press Tab from keyboard and navigate inside the website; Use down/up/left/right arrow keys to navigate to the links available in the page. Note: Avoid using mouse from this step; Keyboard usage is recommended.	Screen reader should read contents from the page clearly; Links should be announced with information on Name, Role and Value of respective links.
Step 4	User the keyboard shortcuts in the attachment (comments column) and perform testing on the website using keyboard only. Additional References: **JAWS Screen Reader:** Use the keyboard shortcuts mentioned in the website below and test the website: https://webaim.org/resources/shortcuts/jaws **NVDA Screen Reader:** https://dequeuniversity.com/screenreaders/nvda-keyboard-shortcuts Important Step: Press INSERT+F7 in NVDA to go to Elements List and select Links Radio Button to check Links listed.	Keyboard shortcuts should announce the respective section of the web page. Pressing INSERT+F7 from NVDA or similar keystrokes in JAWS should display links list clearly on Elements List Display of Screen Readers without errors, and enough information of links should be provided such as Name, Role, and Value. Note: If there are multiple Tables, pressing T should result in going to next table. Similarly use the keyboard shortcuts to navigate in table cells: Ctrl + Alt + down arrow or up arrow or left arrow or right arrow.

After checking few websites, Mark has a list of questions.

- How the links are read from each page and what ARIA properties are required to be added to make it announced by screen reader?
- What is the minimum required text to be announced for the links?
- When a link is announced incorrect, how it impacts users?
- Where to announce if the link will take user to a new page when clicked?

Looking at all these questions, CBK suggested Mark to go through an important formula about links:

"Name Role Value"

He said, this is the mantra for every developer on links and it has to be followed carefully to announce name of the field, role as link, and value as any meaningful sentence about the link while navigating to the links.

Before answering to any questions from Mark, CBK suggested him to read through the complete guidelines of WCAG 2.4.4:

https://www.w3.org/WAI/WCAG21/Understanding/link-purpose-in-context.html

Amazingly, Mark seemed more confident after reading the entire success criterion and is ready to take up the challenge of getting verified on every link of his website pages to make sure that WCAG guidelines are strictly followed.

How the links are read from each page and what ARIA properties are required to be added to make it announced by screen reader?

While speaking to Naren, he understood that "href" is an important content which is getting recognized by screen readers as an attribute that is related to links and screen readers added these links in their "Elements List" dialog box of screen reader (the only visual interactive UI of the screen reader).

In addition to href, title is the most important attribute for every link in the web pages, which get read while navigating from screen readers.

```
href="https://www.engineers-hub.teachable.com" title="Alertbox: teachable learning site—
on web accessibility">
```

This helps the screen reader to announce the Name and Role values.

Recommended Readings:
https://www.nngroup.com/articles/title-attribute/

What is the minimum required text to be announced for the links?
As per webaim.org, there is no minimum allowable length (for short links) or maximum allowable length of link text and these links need to be good enough to explain the purpose. At the same time concise links are designed with an objective of avoiding frustration and confusuion for users with disabilities.

When a link is announced incorrectly, how it impacts users?
Incorrect announcement of links will confuse users most of the times.

Examples:
https://www.addteq.com/products/unstoppable/help/unstoppable-for-confluence/how-to-access-the-elements-list-dialog-of-nvda-in-confluence

Let us see some examples here:

Example of nicely articulated links:

Picture: Image of NVDA elements list displaying links of a demo website.

Example of an elements list which has atleast two links that don't give any informattive details:

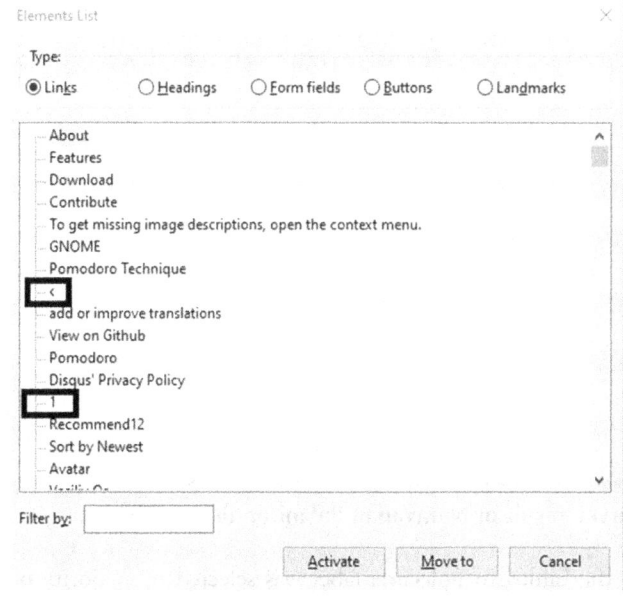

Picture: Image of NVDA elements list displaying links of a demo website in which arrows display the numbers that would create confusion for users with disabilities.

If this is scanned through any automated tests or regular accessibility audit tools, they may still PASS the tests since there are links displayed in elements list. But it doesn't mean they are informative. Hence, this is the primary reason why a manual test only can expose these bugs during a test cycle.

Mark did not stop there. He went on to talk to one of his colleagues, Reena, who has also cleared certifications in International Association of Accessibility Professionals (IAAP). Reena took him toward a new dimension of front-end development:

She said, having a right link with <a> and href value is a good starting point:

<a href="https://engineers-hub.teachable.com/">Engineers Hub Teachable</a>

But it is not good enough yet. You need to have tabindex=0 which helps in screen reader navigation to come to link without any challenges:

<span role="link" tabindex="0" data-href="https:// engineers-hub.teachable.com/">Engineers Hub Teachable </span>

She also warned Mark that he should not get confused with several examples quoted on the Internet since not many of them are right. For example, the recent polls conducted on LinkedIn state that few of the developers are not aware of right attribute for the links and there are different articles talking about different recommendations for the attributes:

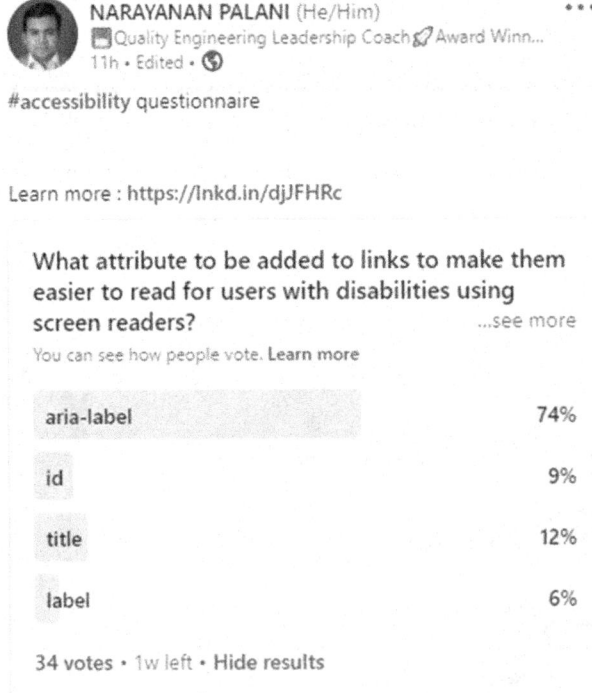

Picture: LinkedIn survey result of Narayanan Palani on link attributes.

Poll Insights: In the LinkedIn poll, aria-label was selected by majority of the engineers but some are confused and selected id and label, which are nowhere helpful to links while getting announced through screen readers.

Now Reena asked Mark whether he knows what is the right set of attributes to go with? He returned an empty face saying, "title probably?" Reena replied, "you are partially right Mark but not 100%."

The real logic of screen readers goes this way:

They search for following attributes in order:

1. aria-labelledby
2. aria-label
3. Texts within <a> and </a>
4. title

Hence your answer of title is a last option if not possible to get any announcement done through first three options.

Reena asked the same question once again for the image-based link implementation and Mark went saying

If the link contains an image, then the logic goes this way:

1. aria-labelledby
2. aria-label
3. alt text within <a> and </a>
4. title

She gave an example implementation in a training website to Mark for reference:

```
<p><a href="https://engineers-hub.teachable.com/p/webaccessibility"> <img src="teacha-
ble.png" alt="Engineers Hub Web Accessibility Best Practices Training"> </a></p>
```

Mark took a deep breath trying to decide on what to implement in grocery website links. He tried few links with title in the past but they were not getting announced right or missing the details at times. Hence went on to ask Naren for testing.

This time he understood the problem and tried the implementation using aria-label:

```
<p>SRF Grocery Store to purchase online and get it delivered next to your door <a
href="https://www.srfgrocery.co.uk" aria-label="Read more about the SRF Grocery Store
Online for exclusive discounts"> Read more... </a> </p><p>
```

This time Naren and Mark tested the link together using NVDA and understood the importance of aria-label while implementing links on any website.

After getting entire links updated with right texts and aria-label, its went for round one of SIT testing with Naren and moved on to CBK for UAT testing and he came back once again with severity 2 defects.

Mark said, "I feel really sorry for him. He has been raising the defects for the sake of raising defects"

But Claire, Engineering Lead, did not buy that idea and set a call between CBK and Mark to find out the reasons behind those defects.

CBK explained some narratives behind the severity 2 justification:

Assume that you are 100% visually impaired and unable to see a little color on your website and it is telling you to simply "click here" then what would you do?

For example:

```
<p> <a href="https://www.srfgrocery.co.uk/products"> click here</a> </p>
```

```
<p> <a href="https://www.srfgrocery.co.uk/help"> Read More</a> </p>
```

It was truly making sense to Claire and she recommended to get some more context to it within the defect description on what to expect in the link texts.

CBK provided a table to Mark which was certainly helpful to understand:

Type	Examples
Good Link Texts	Read More about SRF Grocery Store Click Here to Navigate to Products Page Know More about our Products
Bad Link Texts	Read More Click Here ClickRead Know More More Type Here Move Here Press Here

The next day, Mark fixed most of the links in the following way:

```
<p> <a href="https://www.srfgrocery.co.uk/products"> click here to navigate to products page of SRF Grocery Online</a> </p>
```

```
<p> <a href="https://www.srfgrocery.co.uk/help"> Read More About Help and Support of SRF Grocery Online</a> </p>
```

Lessons Learnt: When in doubt, get it tested; trust your QA and he would never disappoint you.

Where to announce if the link will take user to a new page when clicked?

One of the key questions of Mark was still unanswered and hence he called Nicholas this time to find a right recommendation from WCAG guidelines. Nicholas replied with the link to G201[2] guidelines of WCAG.

Meanwhile, Reena implemented same points in her recent code fix:

```
<p> <a href="https://engineers-hub.teachable.com/p/webaccessibility"> <img src="teachable.png" alt="opens a new window on Engineers Hub Web Accessibility Best Practices Training"> </a> </p>
```

While talking to CBK over call, he mentioned that a link that opens new window should always announce before clicking on the link, hence the user will be prepared to expect a new tab to read the details. Else he or she will end up lost in a new page and struggle to come page to originated page since most of us launch multiple web pages in different tab of browsers.

Lessons Learnt: If the links are taking user to a new web page, new tab, or a new page or a popup or a new section loads within the page as a dynamic load, better to include details in alt property of the link, hence user will be aware of it before the selection.

Now there are two more questions from Mark:

1. How to handle a link when it navigates to external websites?

Talking to Reena was a good choice for Mark and she mentioned, "just add a clear text within alt itself hence user know where they are navigating to":

```
<p> <a href="https://dudocitylearning.co.uk/webaccessibility"> <img src="teachable.png" alt="link opens an external site on Engineers Hub Web Accessibility Best Practices Training"> </a> </p>
```

Alternatively,

```
<p> <a href="https://dudocitylearning.co.uk/webaccessibility"> <img src="teachable.png" alt="Engineers Hub Web Accessibility Best Practices Training (link leads to external website)"> </a> </p>
```

2. Do we need to mention the filetypes when links are provided for the files?

Even Reena had no clue on Mark's questions and they both eventually went into WCAG guidelines to search and find the right solution, which would be appropriate for users using screen readers. This time they found a useful solution in webaim website.[3]

It is important to announce file version in the text format hence user can be prepared to use necessary tools to access the file associated.

```
<ul> <li> <a href="https://srfgrocery.co.uk/brochure"> PDF Version of Product Brochure SRF Grocery </a> </li></ul>
```

Mark is ready for the action!

After looking at the backlog of UI development items, Mark started shaking his head agreeably to Claire stating that he is going to implement accessibility guidelines on links. Claire turned toward Naren and told him to get prepared for the SIT phase since she knows that a QA can break any kind of code to get it tested against accessibility guidelines.

After two days, Naren started testing the links from SRF Grocery pages and found all of them to be working as expected and surprised to realize that he is unable to spot a defect by himself on any of the links updated recently. He found that there is a link which gets highlighted in Yellow color when directed using mouse and he doesn't know what to expect in this case.

Color Contrast Analyzer Tests

He used a color contrast checker[4] in Microsoft Edge to test the links in the latest code of the website and found several issues.

Plugin from Microsoft Edge:

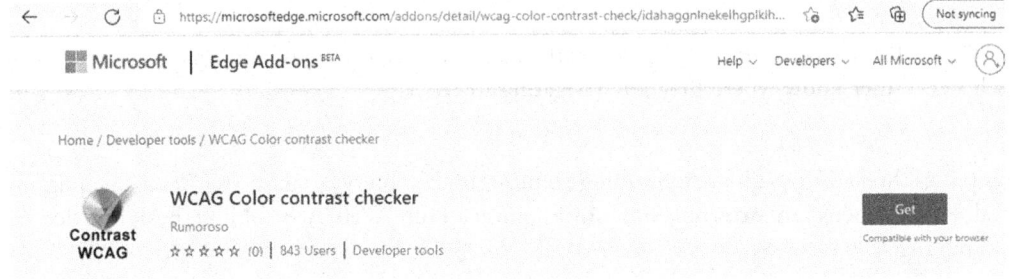

Picture: WCAG Color Contrast Checker as Microsoft Edge Browser's add-on.

Some Errors Displayed during the tests:

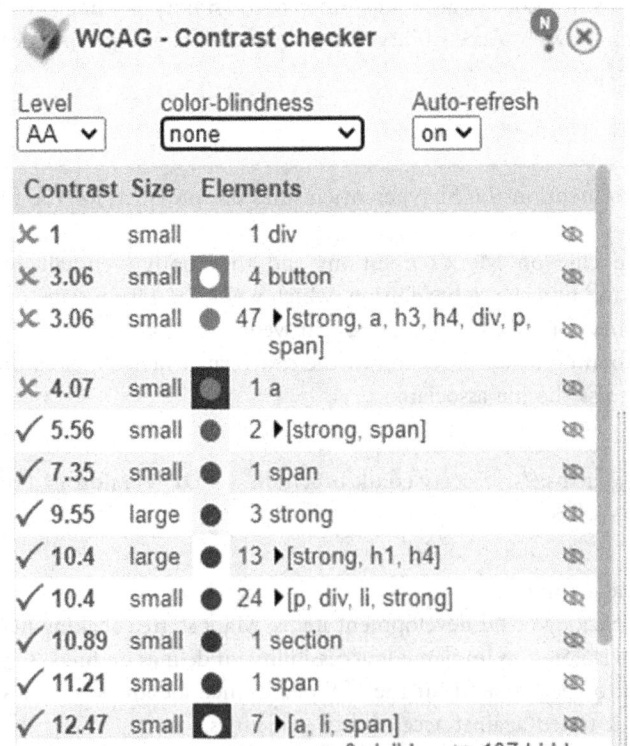

Picture: WCAG Color Contrast Checker Errors of a sample website.

After seeing the Contrast that is less than 3:1, Naren remembered the important guideline: "Color contrast between the link and the text surrounding the link should suppose to be minimum 3:1 and it is recommended to provided further differentiation during a hover over or through a focus when received."

Hence he called CBK to figure out on how to proceed next.

CBK suggested Naren to use one more interesting tool called Funkify-Disability Simulator[5]. After a brief search, Naren landed on to this Google Chrome Plugin and he found the real difficulties user would face when the color is the only representation to any UI object (without having text alternatives).

Lessons Learnt: Color should not be used alone for a visual representation for links. If colors are used to highlight the links when hovering over or moving toward the link, then the color should have a minimum of 3:1 color contrast ratio.

Why Color Contrast Requirements are Important?

Generally, a few developers did not know the importance of 3:1 color contrast standard and as a result there are people that develop applications based on assumptions. One of the recent surveys shows that developers don't know the real reason why color should not be only distinguisher for links. The actual answer is that it impacts users with vision blindness but not many people are aware of it.

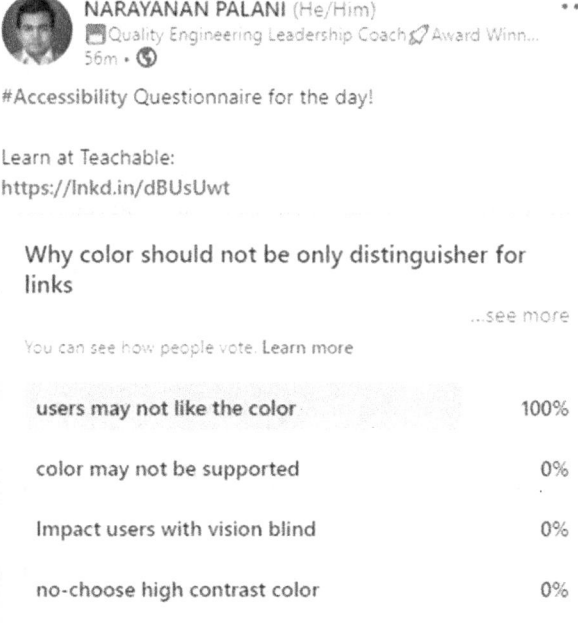

Picture: LinkedIn survey from Narayanan Palani on Colors and Links.

To overcome the challenges, "different color" along with "underline" are the two main styling for links when getting focused. Hence users with partial vision impairment or color blind users can differentiate the focus toward underline of the link since they may not see the color like normal users.

Those who have experienced this accessibility constraint on color contrast realize the importance of the same question when reshared to targeted accessibility engineers group:

Why color should not be the only mode of differentiator for web page links when hover over part of #accessibility testing?

You can see how people vote. **Learn more**

Users dont like some colors	0%
Impact Users with Color Blind	95%
Users find it awkward	5%
Looks unprofessional	0%

Picture: LinkedIn survey from Narayanan Palani on Colors and Page Links.

There are few more best practices used by developers:

- Use a different background color when getting focused or hovered over
- Underline the links along with color differentiation only when link is getting focused or hovered over
- Outlined or provided with a border when link is getting focused or hovered over

Hence it is recommended to use INSERT+F7 in NVDA to verify the links through Elements List to make sure Name, Role, and Value are clearly described for the links.

Once manually checked it can be automated using latest automation tools like CypressIO using JavaScript Programming as an example.

There are two useful plugins widely used by Test Automation Engineers for performing the accessibility audit checks on websites:

What group of plugins help running accessibility tests part of CypressIO automation tests?

...see more

You can see how people vote. **Learn more**

vscode-cy-helper,fiddle	0%
cypress-audit,Cypress-axe	88%
npm-cy,cypress-grep	6%
cypress-repeat,cypress-expect	6%

16 votes • 4d left • Hide results

Picture: LinkedIn survey from Narayanan Palani on CypressIO Plugins.

However, plugins such as cypress-audit and cypress-axe are purely for the reason of accessibility audit and manual testing needs to be performed post-accessibility audit to check the screen reader's behavior.

Link Verification using CypressIO

Write a Feature File using Cucumber

Feature: Verify the Link within OrangeHRM Website to adhere to WCAG Success Criterian 2.4.4 by having link text within html

Scenario: WCAG SC244 Test on Page Links on Footer
Given I open OrangeHRM homepage
Then the link should be provided with url as per WCAG guidelines
And the link should be provided with text as per WCAG guidelines

Write Step Definitions to Verify URL and Text of the Link Provided on the Page

```
Then('the link should be provided with url as per WCAG guidelines', () => {
    loginOrangehrmPage.verifyPageFooterLink()
})

Then('the link should be provided with text as per WCAG guidelines', () => {
    loginOrangehrmPage.verifyFooterLinkTextCheck()
})
```

Add Two Locators and Write a Group of Functions for those Step Definitions

```
const loginFooterLink = '//*[@href="http://www.orangehrm.com"]'
const loginFooterLinkText ='//*[contains(text(),"OrangeHRM, Inc")]'

 verifyPageFooterLink () {
   cy.xpath(loginFooterLink)
       .should('exist')
},
verifyFooterLinkTextCheck () {
   cy.xpath(loginFooterLinkText)
       .should('exist')
}
```

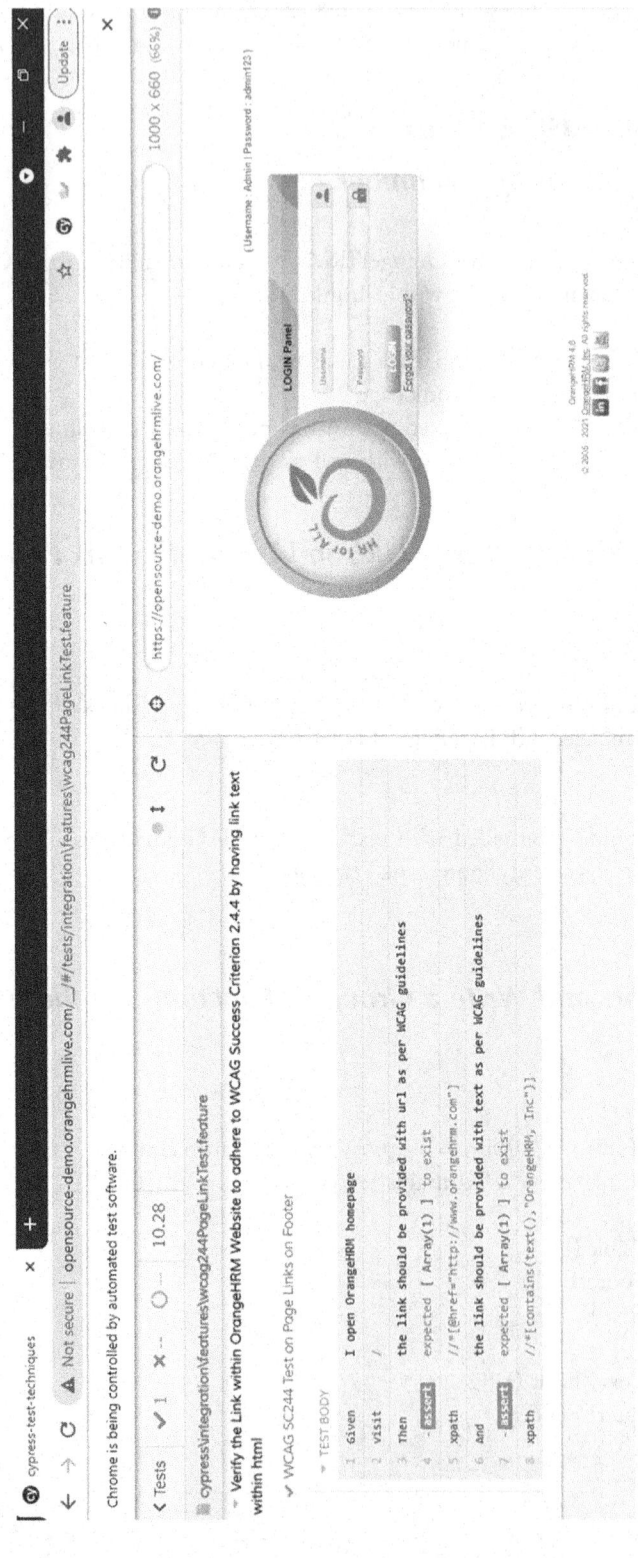

Picture: Cypress Tests control the Chrome browser to interact with website and produce execution results.

After testing using screen readers using NVDA or JAWS or both using two different manual tests, Naren now automated the attributes in Cypress Tests, which runs on Jenkins daily:

This code change can be tracked apart from the pull request on GitHub website[6] for readers to practice the tests.

We learnt about links and different tests involved in verifying their attributes to find defects to have better accessibility in accessing them. But verifying links needs a next step verification through navigation tests by clicking different links from the website. So it is easy to analyze the user behavior to spot any difficulties in announcing the navigations. Let us learn these techniques in the next chapter.

Notes

1. webAccessibilityTestCases. (Accessed 13 December 2021). Retrieved from https://github.com/narayananpalani/webAccessibilityTestCases
2. Title: G201: Giving users advanced warning when opening a new window. (Accessed 12 December 2021). Retrieved from https://www.w3.org/TR/WCAG20-TECHS/G201.html
3. Title: Links and Hypertext. (Accessed 12 December 2021). Retrieved from https://webaim.org/techniques/hypertext/hypertext_links
4. Title: WCAG Color Contrast Checker. (Accessed 12 December 2021). Retrieved from https://microsoftedge.microsoft.com/addons/detail/wcag-color-contrast-check/idahaggnlnekelhgplklhfpchbfdmkjp
5. Title: Funkify – Disability Simulator. (Accessed 12 December 2021). Retrieved from https://chrome.google.com/webstore/detail/funkify-%E2%80%93-disability-simu/ojcijjdchelkddboickefhnbdpeajdjg?hl=en
6. Title: added accessibility automated test for link purpose verification. (Accessed 12 December 2021). Retrieved from https://github.com/narayananpalani/cypress-test-techniques/pull/18

Chapter 10

Website Navigation-based Accessibility Development

Among the navigations of websites, link-based navigations is an aspect where majority of the difficulties experienced for users with disabilities were centered on not announcing the changes on the screen while navigation.

<nav> is most recommended to wrap the elements inside:

```
<nav>
 <ul>
  <li><a xlink:href="home/">Admin</a></li>
  <li><a xlink:href="PIM/">PIM</a></li>
  <li><a xlink:href="leave/">Leave</a></li>
 </ul>
</nav>
```

User Interface:

- Admin
- PIM
- Leave

Picture: Image of User Interface.

If the elements are wrapped with <div>, it is recommended to add a right role as navigation:

```
<div role="navigation">
 <ul>
  <li><a xlink:href="home/">Admin</a></li>
  <li><a xlink:href="PIM/">PIM</a></li>
```

DOI: 10.1201/9781003299431-11

```
<li><a xlink:href="leave/">Leave</a></li>
</ul>
</div>
```

When navigation is updated for role, screen readers and any assistive technologies announce the unordered lists under <ul> very clearly.

Naren thought to initiate testing on sample website to understand how the navigation works, hence he picked up html properties of a sample website, such as for example:

```
<div id="mainMenu" class="menu">
  <ul id="mainMenuFirstLevelUnorderedList" class="main-menu-first-level-unordered-list
main-menu-first-level-unordered-list-width">
  </ul> <!--first level-->
</div>
```

Navigation Menu:

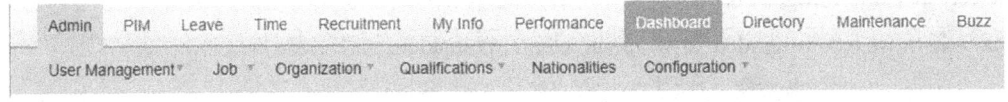

Picture: Image of Navigation Menu.

He knows that role as navigation is missing and he tested it in NVDA and enabled speech viewer option in NVDA to check the announcement. He found a couple of navigation menu items announced as "out of link":

Now that he knows what to update in the properties, hence he chose "inspect element" on the navigation and selected "edit outer html" option to update the role:

```
<div id="mainMenu" class="menu" role="navigation">
  <ul id="mainMenuFirstLevelUnorderedList" class="main-menu-first-level-unordered-list
main-menu-first-level-unordered-list-width">
  </ul> <!-- first level -->

</div>
```

After updating the role, the announcing of text was clearl by NVDA screen reader:

Picture: Image of NVDA Screen Reader's Speech Viewer with couple of texts on "out of list link".

Website Navigation gets Highlighted to Visually Mark the Navigation

After testing the navigation links Naren was super confident on the code until CBK raised a brand new defect in navigation in UAT phase.

CBK walked up to Naren's desk and told him that he wanted to show something interesting on the user navigation. Naren started looking at CBK's desk where ZoomText zoomed the page to 300%. When CBK tried to navigate to Dashboard of the menu items, it all looked good and normal when Naren looked at it. But CBK asked a simple question, "How do I know where my focus is right now?", Naren mentioned that you are on Dashboard menu item but why do you think this is a defect? To Naren's surprise, CBK mentioned that assume that the user is like me with 80% vision loss, how would they understand the navigation when a focused menu is not visually differentiated?

Admin   PIM   Leave   Time   Recruitment   My Info   Performance   Dashboard   Directory   Maintenance   Buzz

Naren understood the core issue that the current page is not highlighted:

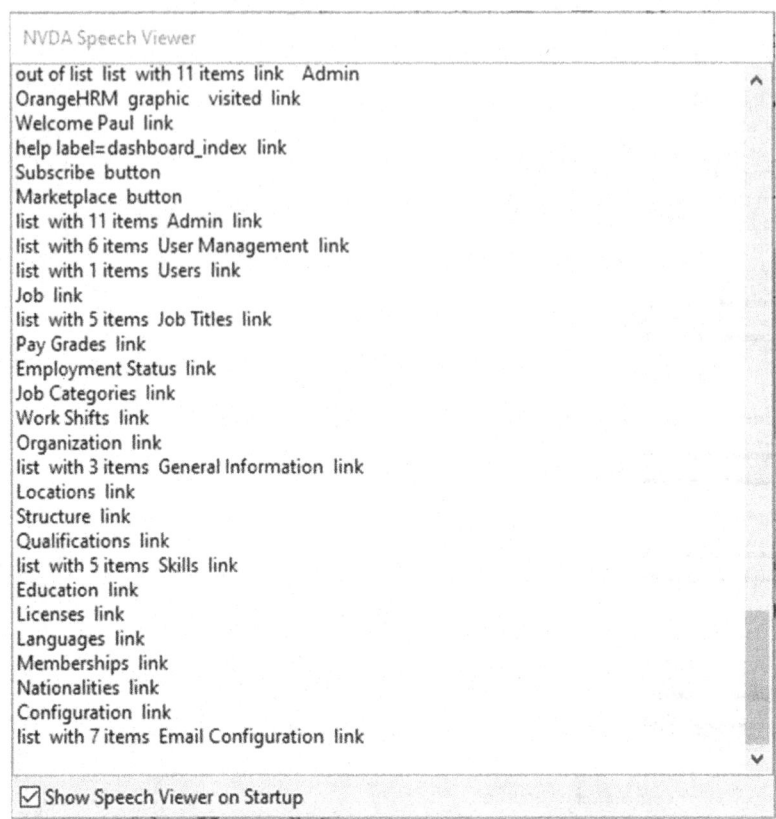

Picture: Image of NVDA Screen Reader's Speech Viewer with link details.

```
<head>
 <title>Demo Page</title>
<style>
 li.current-page {
   outline: red solid 1px;
 }
 </style>
</head>
<ul>
<li><a xlink:href="#">Admin</a></li>
<li><a xlink:href="#">PIM</a></li>
<li><a xlink:href="#">Leave</a></li>
<li><a xlink:href="#">Time</li>
<li><a xlink:href="#">Recruitment</a></li>
<li><a xlink:href="#">My Info</a></li>
<li><a xlink:href="#">Performance</a></li>
```

```
<li><a xlink:href="#">Dashboard</a></li>
<li><a xlink:href="#">Directory</a></li>
<li><a xlink:href="#">Maintenance</a></li>
<li><a xlink:href="#">Buzz</a></li>
</ul>
```

User Interface:

- Admin
- PIM
- Leave
- Time
- Recruitment
- My Info
- Performance
- Dashboard
- Directory
- Maintenance
- Buzz

Picture: User Interface

After seeing this defect, Naren spoke to Mark over the phone and gave an explanation. Mark is not pointing to a code issue that the UI is not highlighting the menu item which is in focus. Hence he made a quick fix in the next 20 minutes.

Highlighting the current page of the website when navigated to it is necessary for users with disability to understand the navigation update:

```
<head>
 <title>Demo Page</title>
<style>
 li.current-page {
   outline: red solid 1px;
 }
 </style>
</head>
<ul>
<li><a xlink:href="#">Admin</a></li>
<li><a xlink:href="#">PIM</a></li>
<li><a xlink:href="#">Leave</a></li>
<li><a xlink:href="#">Time</a></li>
<li><a xlink:href="#">Recruitment</a></li>
<li><a xlink:href="#">My Info</a></li>
<li><a xlink:href="#">Performance</a></li>
<li class="current-page">Dashboard</li>
<li><a xlink:href="#">Directory</a></li>
<li><a xlink:href="#">Maintenance</a></li>
```

```
<li><a xlink:href="#">Buzz</a></li>
</ul>
```

After the fix it shows the UI differentiation clearly:

Admin   PIM   Leave   Time   Recruitment   My Info   Performance   Dashboard   Directory   Maintenance   Buzz

But CBK was not happy with the fix since he found that the "current page" fix was not being announced by screen readers. After seeing his comments, Mark tried to implement an aria-label to see if it gets announced:

```
<head>
 <title>Demo Page</title>
 <style>
  li.current-page {
   outline: red solid 1px;
  }
 </style>
</head>
<ul>
<li><a xlink:href="#">Admin</a></li>
<li><a xlink:href="#">PIM</a></li>
<li><a xlink:href="#">Leave</a></li>
<li><a xlink:href="#">Time</li>
<li><a xlink:href="#">Recruitment</a></li>
<li><a xlink:href="#">My Info</a></li>
<li><a xlink:href="#">Performance</a></li>
<li class="current-page">
    <a xlink:href="#Dashboard" aria-label="Current page: Dashboard">
      Dashboard
    </a>
</li>
<li><a xlink:href="#">Directory</a></li>
<li><a xlink:href="#">Maintenance</a></li>
<li><a xlink:href="#">Buzz</a></li>
</ul>
```

In addition to the above, CBK mentioned that aria-label is a key that helps in reading the details of links. But the challenge is that aria-label attribute overrides the link's texts, which are provided in DOM elements. So it is highly advisable to copy the same content of link text inside aria-label so that the information is not missed.

After the recent implementation, CBK found that the announcement was clear to read on Current Page when navigating to particular menu item. Alternatively span can be used with visually hidden class as well.

Post discussion with CBK, our front-end engineer Mark concluded to use span with visually hidden features and updated both current-page class and css attribute as below:

```
<head>
<title>Engineers Hub Teachable Website</title>
<style>
 .visually-hidden {
 position: absolute;
 clip: rect(0 0 0 0);
 border: 0;
 height: 1px; margin: -1px;
 overflow: hidden;
 padding: 0
 width: 1px;
 white-space: nowrap;
 }
 li.current-page {
 outline: 1px solid red;
 }
</style>
</head>
<body>
<nav>
<ul>
<li><a xlink:href="#">Admin</a></li>
<li><a xlink:href="#">PIM</a></li>
<li><a xlink:href="#">Leave</a></li>
<li><a xlink:href="#">Time</li>
<li><a xlink:href="#">Recruitment</a></li>
<li><a xlink:href="#">My Info</a></li>
<li><a xlink:href="#">Performance</a></li>
<li class="current-page">
   <span class="visually-hidden">Current page: </span>Dashboard
</li>
<li><a xlink:href="#">Directory</a></li>
<li><a xlink:href="#">Maintenance</a></li>
<li><a xlink:href="#">Buzz</a></li>
</ul>
</nav>
</body>
```

Try using the code above in the w3schools website to learn the UI display: https://www.w3schools.com/html/tryit.asp?filename=tryhtml_basic

This code has helped the UI focus in following way:

- Admin
- PIM
- Leave
- Time
- Recruitment
- My Info
- Performance
- Dashboard
- Directory
- Maintenance
- Buzz

Picture: User Interface with focus on Dashboard.

Lessons Learnt: aria-label, aria-labelledby, or class=visually-hidden are essential to announce the current page when navigated to particular menu item since it helps screen reader with the announcement.

After learning these key lessons from CBK, Naren was keen to get another opportunity to test navigations of web pages and this time it was their organization's HR website, which is going through new feature upgradations recently. So he took some time to verify the leave related pages and spotted a wonderful bug.

```
<h1>[HR Home Page]</h1>

<h2>Table of Contents</h2>
<ul>
<li><a xlink:href="#Salary">Salary</a></li>
<li><a xlink:href="#Sick Leave">Sick Leave</a></li>
<li><a xlink:href="#Paternity Leave">Paternity Leave</a></li>
<li><a xlink:href="#Loss of Pay">Loss of Pay</a></li>
</ul>

<div>[Book Leaves]</div>


<h1>[Your Leave History]</h1>

<h2>Table of Contents</h2>
<ul>
<li><a xlink:href="#Loss of Pay">Loss of Pay</a></li>
<li><a xlink:href="#Salary">Salary</a></li>
<li><a xlink:href="#Paternity Leave">Paternity Leave</a></li>
<li><a xlink:href="#Sick Leave">Sick Leave</a></li>
</ul>

<div>[Cancel or Amend Leaves]</div>
```

User Interface:

[HR Home Page]

Table of Contents

- Salary
- Sick Leave
- Paternity Leave
- Loss of Pay

[Book Leaves]

[Your Leave History]

Table of Contents

- Loss of Pay
- Salary
- Paternity Leave
- Sick Leave

[Cancel or Amend Leaves]

Picture: User Interface with different headings and subheadings.

"Do you spot any defect by the look of the html elements above?" he asked Mark and eventually Mark had no clue on why Naren is telling the whole HR leave pages have a defect. But Naren narrated following the key description:

"When I navigated to HR Home Page it was showing Salary, Sick Leave, Paternity Leave and Loss of Pay as Table of Contents and the same order is changed in 'Your Leave History' page. If a user reads this page, they will easily get distracted due to this inconsistency."

After the latest fix, Naren closed the defect after verifying the html elements as below:

```
<h1>[HR Home Page]</h1>

<h2>Table of Contents</h2>
<ul>
<li><a xlink:href="#Salary">Salary</a></li>
<li><a xlink:href="#Sick Leave">Sick Leave</a></li>
<li><a xlink:href="#Paternity Leave">Paternity Leave</a></li>
<li><a xlink:href="#Loss of Pay">Loss of Pay</a></li>
</ul>
```

```
<div>[Book Leaves]</div>


<h1>[Your Leave History]</h1>

<h2>Table of Contents</h2>
<ul>
<li><a xlink:href="#Salary">Salary</a></li>
<li><a xlink:href="#Sick Leave">Sick Leave</a></li>
<li><a xlink:href="#Paternity Leave">Paternity Leave</a></li>
<li><a xlink:href="#Loss of Pay">Loss of Pay</a></li>
</ul>

<div>[Cancel or Amend Leaves]</div>
```

User Interface:

[HR Home Page]

Table of Contents

- Salary
- Sick Leave
- Paternity Leave
- Loss of Pay

[Book Leaves]

[Your Leave History]

Table of Contents

- Salary
- Sick Leave
- Paternity Leave
- Loss of Pay

[Cancel or Amend Leaves]

Picture: User Interface with different headings and subheadings.

Mark learnt a key lesson here:

Consistency of navigation through Table of Contents or any list provided with links on the website are important and aligned across the pages.

Positive Tabindex Causes Problems

Similar to the lessons of skip link, Mark tried using tabindex=1 along with tabindex=2 and tabindex=3 for consecutive links on the web page but they all led to significant confusion while CBK was testing using screen readers he mentioned. The primary reason was that the reading order and tab order got messed up with positive tabindex used.

Lessons Learnt:
Tabindex=0 is standard practice in majority of the websites for a normal way of navigation from one to another in order to maintain an aligned navigation using keyboard TAB key navigation. Alternatively the element need not be included in tab order (items other than links) can have tabindex= – 1 in order to get the element focusable by script but doesn't come under the keyboard focus order.

Keyboard Shortcuts Customization and Website Accessibility

While discussing about the features of latest options to let customers choose keyboard shortcuts to book leaves in the portal by pressing L button led to CBK raising a defect on the feature.

Claire eventually got disappointed to see her own leave page go to Book Leave button whenever she tried to amend the leave reason text box and she entered L part of her paragraph. When she mentioned this to CBK, he said he is aware of these kind of difficulties cause by website when keyboard shortcuts are introduced, hence the only way is to provide another feature to disable the keyboard shortcuts through settings (like gmail settings feature of keyboard shortcuts which let users to turn "keyboard shortcuts off or on").

Single Page Navigation Techniques or Better Navigation Accessibility Inside or within a Web Page

Naren called CBK for a defect status and eventually remembered to ask his questions on "navigation within web pages" since he knows how to test between the pages right now but not sure how users with vision blindness navigate within single web page when there are hundreds of links and images. To his surprise, CBK answered one word, that is "Skip Link."

After searching few code examples, Naren learnt that majority of the users with disability try to navigate to main content of the page when the page is loaded. But it is not possible immediately since there are plenteous of links or tabs at headers in many websites since they use the feature purely written for accessibility known as "Skip Navigation Link" feature in this format:

```
<div id="skipnav"><a xlink:href="#mainContent">Skip navigation</a></div>

<!-- Header Section -->

<main id="mainContent" tabindex="-1">
   <!-- Key contents or actions of the web page -->
</main>
```

Basically, Tab navigation of the web page announces "skip navigation" when the page is loaded hence user gets an option to skip all the header sections to go directly to main content by one keyboard action (by pressing "Enter" when announced as skip navigation) but this feature is not visible in some of the websites until navigated through keyboard focus since the feature is purely hidden in html elements level and used only when interacted through screen readers with key-strokes such as "Tab."

Before all these, a key lesson to be learnt:

> "Skip navigation should be the first focused item when the website is loaded and announced through screen readers"

The simple reason is that, when skip navigation option is itself announced later, user has to try navigation keystrokes such as "Tab" key to navigate to several objects to reach to skip navigation, which is not a good experience.

Lessons Learnt:
Make sure to write skip navigation code within the body of your web page in such a way that loading or reloading the web page result in announcing skip navigation as a first option for users through assistive technologies such as screen readers.

Example:

```
<body>
<div id="skipnav"><a xlink:href="#mainContent">Skip navigation</a></div>

<!-- Header Section -->

<main id="mainContent" tabindex="-1">
  <!-- Key contents or actions of the web page -->
</main>
```

After seeing this code, Mark updated his css attributes to skip link as below:

```
<head>
 <title>Engineers Hub Teachable Website</title>
 <style>
  #skipnav a {
   position: absolute;
   clip: rect(0 0 0 0);
   border: 0;
   height: 1px; margin: -1px;
   overflow: hidden;
   padding: 0
   width: 1px;
   white-space: nowrap;
  }
```

```
#skipnav a:focus {
    clip:auto;
    left:0;
    top:0;
    width:100%;
    height:auto;
    margin:0;
    padding:10px 0;
    background:#fdf6e7;
    border:2px solid #990000;
    border-left:none;
    border-right:none;
    text-align:center;
    font-weight:bold;
    color:#990000;
    }
  </style>
</head>
<body>
  <div id="skipnav"><a xlink:href="#mainContent">Skip navigation</a></div>
  <!-- document banner, navigation, etc. -->
  <main id="mainContent" tabindex="-1">
    <h1>After pressing the skip link option through keyboard,it brings the user here.</h1>
    <!-- contents within main content -->
  </main>
  <!-- content on the website -->
</body>
```

While learning these techniques, Naren happened to discuss this with Mark and co-incidently he shared one of the bitter experience with the display:none feature earlier. Yes, Mark did try an option to hide the skip link for one of their web pages by including display:none confiugtion but it end up not getting announced by screen reader, hence he removed it immediately.

There are two important choices for developers:

1. Bring the skip link visible when keyboard is focused (hence other times it is hidden and not visible)
2. Skip link is visible constantly hence normal users or users with partial vision impairment see this link all the time on top of the web page and also available as a first focusable item when navigated post page load.

As a crucial test on web accessibility, we learn about navigation and link-based best practices in this chapter. Let us learn about table-based accessibility tests in the next chapter to understand how tables can be announced through screen readers when interacting with websites.

Chapter 11

Website Tables-based Accessibility Development

Usually, Naren tests tables with keyboard shortcuts, such as Ctrl+Alt+Arrow Keys and as Ctrl+ Alt+Right arrow to navigate within the table and go from one cell to another cell (right arrow helps to move from left to right). Similarly keystroke T is used to move between one table to other.

But he was so desperate to understand on how users with disabilities access these tables when they have vision impairments, such as 70% or above.

Table with Caption

Purpose of the table and details given in the table should be described in a separate caption section of the html elements to help users with disabilities. Hence screen readers realize the caption to announce first while navigating to the tables.

Adding captions to the table helps in reading details about the table in screen readers before getting on to the row and columns.

Cricket Score Table					
Team A			Team B		
Sachin	Ganguly	Dhoni	Laura	Pollock	Smith
Test 1 2	17	51	55	100	3
Test 2 28	26	38	27	24	24
Test 3 103	55	6	23	305	101

Picture: Image with table contents of "Cricket Score Table".

DOI: 10.1201/9781003299431-12

HTML code:

```
<table class="data complex">
 <caption>
  Cricket Score Table
 </caption>
 <thead>
  <tr>
   <td rowspan="2"></td>
   <th colspan="3" scope="colgroup">Team A</th>
   <th colspan="3" scope="colgroup">Team B</th>
  </tr>
  <tr>
   <th scope="col">Sachin</th>
   <th scope="col">Ganguly</th>
   <th scope="col">Dhoni</th>
   <th scope="col">Laura</th>
   <th scope="col">Pollock</th>
   <th scope="col">Smith</th>
  </tr>
 </thead>
 <tbody>
  <tr>
   <th scope="row">Test 1</th>
   <td>2</td>
   <td>17</td>
   <td>51</td>
   <td>55</td>
   <td>100</td>
   <td>3</td>
  </tr>
  <tr>
   <th scope="row">Test 2</th>
   <td>28</td>
   <td>26</td>
   <td>38</td>
   <td>27</td>
   <td>24</td>
   <td>24</td>
  </tr>
  <tr>
   <th scope="row">Test 3</th>
   <td>103</td>
   <td>55</td>
   <td>6</td>
   <td>23</td>
```

```
    <td>305</td>
    <td>101</td>
  </tr>
 </tbody>
</table>
```

While using screen reader, it is read clearly with caption:

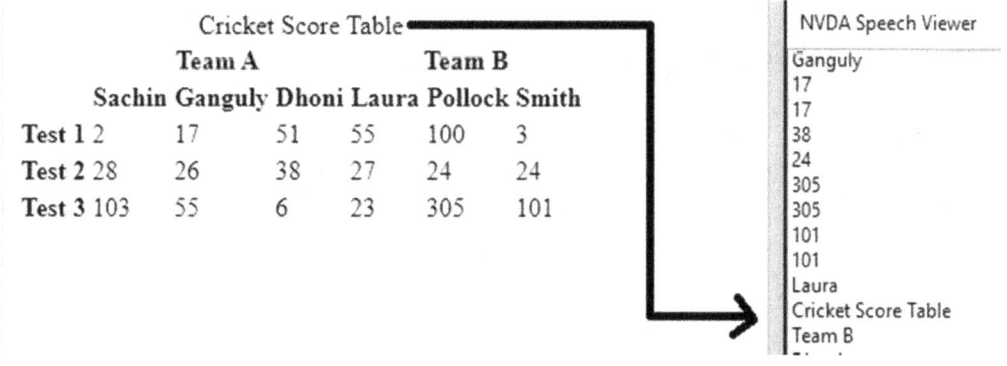

Picture: Image of the table and NVDA Speech Viewer that announces the contents of table.

What if the caption is missing in the table?

Table without caption will create a confusion on the table details:

	Team A			Team B	
	Sachin	Ganguly	Dhoni	Laura	Pollock	Smith
Test 1 2	17	51	55	100	3
Test 2 28	26	38	27	24	24
Test 3 103	55	6	23	305	101

Picture: Image of the table contains several numbers involved in cricket score without mentioning any title for the table.

Table with aria-label

Usually caption texts are visible to users but if developer prefers to give text as invisible content and usable only to screen reader, it is recommended to use aria-label as below:

```
<table class="data complex" aria-label="Table of Cricket Scores">
 <caption>
  Cricket Score Table
 </caption>
```

```
<thead>
 <tr>
  <td rowspan="2"></td>
  <th colspan="3" scope="colgroup">Team A</th>
  <th colspan="3" scope="colgroup">Team B</th>
 </tr>
 <tr>
  <th scope="col">Sachin</th>
  <th scope="col">Ganguly</th>
  <th scope="col">Dhoni</th>
  <th scope="col">Laura</th>
  <th scope="col">Pollock</th>
  <th scope="col">Smith</th>
 </tr>
</thead>
<tbody>
 <tr>
  <th scope="row">Test 1</th>
  <td>2</td>
  <td>17</td>
  <td>51</td>
  <td>55</td>
  <td>100</td>
  <td>3</td>
 </tr>
 <tr>
  <th scope="row">Test 2</th>
  <td>28</td>
  <td>26</td>
  <td>38</td>
  <td>27</td>
  <td>24</td>
  <td>24</td>
 </tr>
 <tr>
  <th scope="row">Test 3</th>
  <td>103</td>
  <td>55</td>
  <td>6</td>
  <td>23</td>
  <td>305</td>
  <td>101</td>
 </tr>
</tbody>
</table>
```

Table with aria-labelledby

Some developers prefer aria-labelledby at table level property since majority of the screen readers search for aria-labelledby as a first item to find and get it announced:

```
<table aria-labelledby="Table of Cricket Scores of two teams">
<caption>
 Cricket Score Table
</caption>
<thead>
  <tr>
   <td rowspan="2"></td>
   <th colspan="3" scope="colgroup">Team A</th>
   <th colspan="3" scope="colgroup">Team B</th>
  </tr>
  <tr>
   <th scope="col">Sachin</th>
   <th scope="col">Ganguly</th>
   <th scope="col">Dhoni</th>
   <th scope="col">Laura</th>
   <th scope="col">Pollock</th>
   <th scope="col">Smith</th>
  </tr>
</thead>
  <tbody>
  <tr>
   <th scope="row">Test 1</th>
   <td>2</td>
   <td>17</td>
   <td>51</td>
   <td>55</td>
   <td>100</td>
   <td>3</td>
  </tr>
  <tr>
   <th scope="row">Test 2</th>
   <td>28</td>
   <td>26</td>
   <td>38</td>
   <td>27</td>
   <td>24</td>
   <td>24</td>
  </tr>
  <tr>
   <th scope="row">Test 3</th>
```

```
    <td>103</td>
    <td>55</td>
    <td>6</td>
    <td>23</td>
    <td>305</td>
    <td>101</td>
  </tr>
 </tbody>
</table>
```

Table with Row Group

Usually tables with multiple rows and columns are very difficult to read for users with vision loss since there are different numbers to read for different rows and columns at times. In addition, it is recommended to have <th> to mark headers for both row header and column headers, which will help users with partial visibility to differentiate the values and headers. Introducing row group, column group, row header, and column header helps readers in clear differentiation:

		Cricket Score Table					
		Team A			**Team B**		
		Sachin	**Ganguly**	**Dhoni**	**Laura**	**Pollock**	**Smith**
Foreign Tours	**Test 1**	2	17	51	55	100	3
Foreign Tours	**Test 2**	28	26	38	27	24	24
Local Tours	**Test 3**	103	55	6	23	305	101

Picture: Image of the table with three types of tours.

Table code with row group and column group:

```
<table class="data complex" aria-label="Table of Cricket Scores">
<caption>
 Cricket Score Table
</caption>
<thead>
  <tr>
  <td rowspan="2"></td>
  <th colspan="3" scope="colgroup">Team A</th>
  <th colspan="3" scope="colgroup">Team B</th>
  </tr>
  <tr>
  <th scope="col">Sachin</th>
  <th scope="col">Ganguly</th>
  <th scope="col">Dhoni</th>
  <th scope="col">Laura</th>
```

```
      <th scope="col">Pollock</th>
      <th scope="col">Smith</th>
    </tr>
  </thead>
  <tbody>
    <tr>
    <th rowspan="1" scope="rowgroup">Foreign Tours</th>
    <th scope="row">Test 1</th>
    <td>2</td>
    <td>17</td>
    <td>51</td>
    <td>55</td>
    <td>100</td>
    <td>3</td>
    </tr>
    <tr>
    <th rowspan="1" scope="rowgroup">Foreign Tours</th>
    <th scope="row">Test 2</th>
    <td>28</td>
    <td>26</td>
    <td>38</td>
    <td>27</td>
    <td>24</td>
    <td>24</td>
    </tr>
    <tr>
    <th rowspan="2" scope="rowgroup">Local Tours</th>
    <th scope="row">Test 3</th>
    <td>103</td>
    <td>55</td>
    <td>6</td>
    <td>23</td>
    <td>305</td>
    <td>101</td>
    </tr>
  </tbody>
</table>
```

Table with Summary

When any websites are developed prior to HTML5, it is highly recommended to add summary to the table section to get concise information about the tables to be announced through screen readers:

```
<table class="cricket_scores" summary="This table lists the members of cricket team with
their score in each test match.">
 <caption>
  Cricket Score Table
 </caption>
<thead>
  <tr>
   <td rowspan="2"></td>
   <th colspan="3" scope="colgroup">Team A</th>
   <th colspan="3" scope="colgroup">Team B</th>
  </tr>
  <tr>
   <th scope="col">Sachin</th>
   <th scope="col">Ganguly</th>
   <th scope="col">Dhoni</th>
   <th scope="col">Laura</th>
   <th scope="col">Pollock</th>
   <th scope="col">Smith</th>
  </tr>
</thead>
 <tbody>
  <tr>
   <th scope="row">Test 1</th>
   <td>2</td>
   <td>17</td>
   <td>51</td>
   <td>55</td>
   <td>100</td>
   <td>3</td>
  </tr>
  <tr>
   <th scope="row">Test 2</th>
   <td>28</td>
   <td>26</td>
   <td>38</td>
   <td>27</td>
   <td>24</td>
   <td>24</td>
  </tr>
  <tr>
   <th scope="row">Test 3</th>
   <td>103</td>
   <td>55</td>
   <td>6</td>
   <td>23</td>
   <td>305</td>
```

```
      <td>101</td>
    </tr>
  </tbody>
</table>
```

Table with Table Description

As an alternative to summary of the table, table description can be used to provide one or two sentences about the table provided in web page:

```
<p id="table-description">This table lists the members of the cricket team with scores from each test match</p>
<table aria-describedby="table-description">
  <caption>
  Cricket Score Table
  </caption>
<thead>
    <tr>
    <td rowspan="2"></td>
    <th colspan="3" scope="colgroup">Team A</th>
    <th colspan="3" scope="colgroup">Team B</th>
    </tr>
    <tr>
    <th scope="col">Sachin</th>
    <th scope="col">Ganguly</th>
    <th scope="col">Dhoni</th>
    <th scope="col">Laura</th>
    <th scope="col">Pollock</th>
    <th scope="col">Smith</th>
    </tr>
</thead>
<tbody>
    <tr>
    <th scope="row">Test 1</th>
    <td>2</td>
    <td>17</td>
    <td>51</td>
    <td>55</td>
    <td>100</td>
    <td>3</td>
    </tr>
    <tr>
    <th scope="row">Test 2</th>
    <td>28</td>
```

```
    <td>26</td>
    <td>38</td>
    <td>27</td>
    <td>24</td>
    <td>24</td>
  </tr>
  <tr>
    <th scope="row">Test 3</th>
    <td>103</td>
    <td>55</td>
    <td>6</td>
    <td>23</td>
    <td>305</td>
    <td>101</td>
  </tr>
 </tbody>
</table>
```

Table with Table Fig Caption

It is also possible to use table-figcaption to provide detailed summary of the table:

This table lists the members of the cricket team with scores from each test match

		Cricket Score Table			
	Team A			Team B	
	Sachin	Ganguly	Dhoni	Laura	Pollock	Smith
Test 1	2	17	51	55	100	3
Test 2	28	26	38	27	24	24
Test 3	103	55	6	23	305	101

Picture: Image of cricket score table of three different tests.

HTML code:

```
<figure>
<figcaption id="table-figcaption">This table lists the members of the cricket team with scores from each test match</figcaption>

<table aria-describedby="table-figcaption">
 <caption>
   Cricket Score Table
 </caption>
```

```
<thead>
  <tr>
   <td rowspan="2"></td>
   <th colspan="3" scope="colgroup">Team A</th>
   <th colspan="3" scope="colgroup">Team B</th>
  </tr>
  <tr>
   <th scope="col">Sachin</th>
   <th scope="col">Ganguly</th>
   <th scope="col">Dhoni</th>
   <th scope="col">Laura</th>
   <th scope="col">Pollock</th>
   <th scope="col">Smith</th>
  </tr>
</thead>
 <tbody>
  <tr>
   <th scope="row">Test 1</th>
   <td>2</td>
   <td>17</td>
   <td>51</td>
   <td>55</td>
   <td>100</td>
   <td>3</td>
  </tr>
  <tr>
   <th scope="row">Test 2</th>
   <td>28</td>
   <td>26</td>
   <td>38</td>
   <td>27</td>
   <td>24</td>
   <td>24</td>
  </tr>
  <tr>
   <th scope="row">Test 3</th>
   <td>103</td>
   <td>55</td>
   <td>6</td>
   <td>23</td>
   <td>305</td>
   <td>101</td>
  </tr>
 </tbody>
</table>
</figure>
```

Limitations with Tables

Tables are not displayed appropriately in mobile device-based browsers and apps, hence it will be difficult for readers to use assistive technologies on a mobile device to read tables. When developers create HTML structures without proper recommended mechanisms to include <table> <tr> and <td> structures, it will create difficulties while using screen readers on the tables.

Interesting Defects Captured when Visually Hidden Placed Inside Caption

When mark developed the first set of code, Naren was testing the html code below and found that the table is read by screen readers with incorrect row numbers:

```
<head>
 <title>Engineers-Hub Teachable Website</title>
</head>
<body>

<p id="table-description" class="visually-hidden">This table lists the members of the cricket team with scores from each test match</p>

<table aria-describedby="table-description">
 <caption>
  Cricket Score Table
  <style>
  .visually-hidden {
    position: absolute;
    clip: rect(0 0 0 0);
    border: 0;
    height: 1px; margin: -1px;
    overflow: hidden;
    padding: 0;
    width: 1px;
    white-space: nowrap;
  }
  li.current-page {
    outline: 1px solid red;
  }
  </style>
 </caption>
 <thead>
   <tr>
    <td rowspan="2"></td>
```

```
    <th colspan="3" scope="colgroup">Team A</th>
    <th colspan="3" scope="colgroup">Team B</th>
  </tr>
  <tr>
    <th scope="col">Sachin</th>
    <th scope="col">Ganguly</th>
    <th scope="col">Dhoni</th>
    <th scope="col">Laura</th>
    <th scope="col">Pollock</th>
    <th scope="col">Smith</th>
  </tr>
</thead>
<tbody>
  <tr>
    <th scope="row">Test 1</th>
    <td>2</td>
    <td>17</td>
    <td>51</td>
    <td>55</td>
    <td>100</td>
    <td>3</td>
  </tr>
  <tr>
    <th scope="row">Test 2</th>
    <td>28</td>
    <td>26</td>
    <td>38</td>
    <td>27</td>
    <td>24</td>
    <td>24</td>
  </tr>
  <tr>
    <th scope="row">Test 3</th>
    <td>103</td>
    <td>55</td>
    <td>6</td>
    <td>23</td>
    <td>305</td>
    <td>101</td>
  </tr>
  </tbody>
</table>
</body>
```

After seeing the defect, Mark understood that the visually hidden properties inside caption have created the poor behavior on screen readers.

Table with Table Description Visually Hidden

After Mark provided the right fix, Naren sensed the right screen reader behavior with html elements below:

```
<head>
  <title>Engineers-Hub Teachable Website</title>
  <style>
    .visually-hidden {
      position: absolute;
      clip: rect(0 0 0 0);
      border: 0;
      height: 1px; margin: -1px;
      overflow: hidden;
      padding: 0
      width: 1px;
      white-space: nowrap;
    }
    li.current-page {
      outline: 1px solid red;
    }
  </style>
</head>
<body>

<p id="table-description" class="visually-hidden">This table lists the members of the cricket team with scores from each test match</p>

<table aria-describedby="table-description">
<caption>
  Cricket Score Table
</caption>
<thead>
  <tr>
    <td rowspan="2"></td>
    <th colspan="3" scope="colgroup">Team A</th>
    <th colspan="3" scope="colgroup">Team B</th>
  </tr>
  <tr>
    <th scope="col">Sachin</th>
    <th scope="col">Ganguly</th>
    <th scope="col">Dhoni</th>
```

```
      <th scope="col">Laura</th>
      <th scope="col">Pollock</th>
      <th scope="col">Smith</th>
    </tr>
  </thead>
  <tbody>
    <tr>
    <th scope="row">Test 1</th>
    <td>2</td>
    <td>17</td>
    <td>51</td>
    <td>55</td>
    <td>100</td>
    <td>3</td>
    </tr>
    <tr>
    <th scope="row">Test 2</th>
    <td>28</td>
    <td>26</td>
    <td>38</td>
    <td>27</td>
    <td>24</td>
    <td>24</td>
    </tr>
    <tr>
    <th scope="row">Test 3</th>
    <td>103</td>
    <td>55</td>
    <td>6</td>
    <td>23</td>
    <td>305</td>
    <td>101</td>
    </tr>
  </tbody>
</table>
</body>
```

Lessons Learnt: Never add visually hidden inside caption of table html elements

Post tables testing, Naren and Mark get together for a sprint review meeting; Mark said he discovered a wonderful website[1] lately, which has some great examples available to build the tables with better accessibility friendly features.

The moral of the story is that table may look correct but need not be accessibility compliant all the time and it is at risk of accessibility defects in most of the areas when any data are represented in table format.

We learnt about testing tables against accessibility guidelines but we are yet to learn about lists and their accessibility adherence while testing websites. Let us learn those list-based accessibility checks in the next chapter.

Note

1. Title: Resources For Building Accessible Tables. (Accessed 12 December 2021). Retrieved from https://www.digitala11y.com/resources-for-building-accessible-tables/

Chapter 12

Website Lists-based Accessibility Development

Mark, our front-end engineer, thought of using simple paragraphs with <br> initially. But Naren hinted that it's not going to work out good for screen readers, as users with disabilities are expected to listen to list of items announcement when they navigate to any type of lists.

Sample Code[1]:

```
<!DOCTYPE html>
<html>
<body>

<h2>An Unordered HTML List</h2>

<ul>
 <li>Selenium</li>
 <li>Cypress</li>
 <li>UFT</li>
</ul>

<h2>An Ordered HTML List</h2>

<ol>
 <li>Selenium</li>
 <li>Cypress</li>
 <li>UFT</li>
</ol>

<h2>The dl, dd, and dt elements</h2>
```

DOI: 10.1201/9781003299431-13

```
<p>These three elements are used to create a description list:</p>

<dl>
 <dt>Selenium</dt>
 <dd>Selenium Java Programming Framework</dd>
 <dd>WebdriverIO Javascript Programming Framework</dd>
 <dd>Selenium DotNet Programming Framework</dd>
 <dt>Cypress</dt>
 <dd>Cypress Javascript Programming Framework</dd>
</dl>

</body>
</html>
```

When running this code, it can be seen as the screenshot below:

An Unordered HTML List

- Selenium
- Cypress
- UFT

An Ordered HTML List

1. Selenium
2. Cypress
3. UFT

The dl, dd, and dt elements

These three elements are used to create a description list:

Selenium
  Selenium Java Programming Framework
  WebdriverIO Javascript Programming Framework
  Selenium DotNet Programming Framework
Cypress
  Cypress Javascript Programming Framework

Picture: Image of lists from sample website.

Basically, unordered lists, ordered lists, and definition lists are announced clearly in screen readers when navigated through keyboard above, below, left, or right keys. Instead of choosing any of these three types, listing down the paragraphs with <br> will not help those users with screen readers. This is a key lesson when testing any lists in the websites.

Now that Naren, while testing screen readers, had a doubt that there is no specific keyboard shortcut available to navigate to lists on the website, he called CBK once again and CBK shared just one command this time, that too only for JAWS:

INSERT+CONTROL+L

Yes, that's right. He mentioned that JAWS is the only tool that helps with a keyboard shortcut that shows all tables list. But rest of the screen readers help in navigating from one list to other list with the help of keyboard shortcut:

L

As an exception, if you are using MacBook to navigate inside Safari browser, try using the shortcut as

Control+Alt+Command+X

Naren tried to navigate from one list to next using L shortcut but he wanted to navigate within the list from one item to next and he did not find a way out. As usual, he tried reaching CBK and CBK shared another command for navigation within the list this time:

I

That's right. Pressing "I" helps in navigating from one list item to next list item. Everyone knows the value of CBK being a senior accessibility consultant in the team, with his inspirational journey full of struggles with 70% vision loss.

We learnt about short tips on lists testing against accessibility guidelines in this chapter, and the next step is to verify page break navigation against accessibility guidelines.

Note

1. Title: w3schools code. (Accessed 12 December 2021). Retrieved from https://www.w3schools.com/html/tryit.asp?filename=tryhtml_lists_intro

Chapter 13

Website Page Media—Page Break-based Accessibility Development

CBK and Naren were due to test a new release in which the terms and conditions are provided as a PDF version on the website. CBK mentioned that reading a PDF version or a digital version of the book is always not straightforward for him since he can reach the page using keystrokes but reading the digital print version differs from book to book on the basis of their availability to read through screen reader interactions.

Hence they both decided to test some of the existing features from Google Play before getting on to actual website for the terms and conditions for testing. While navigating to Google Play, they found some interesting features in it.

Let us look at the sample PDF of Google Play to read a test automation book on "selenium webdriver."[2]

While navigating to free sample as PDF invoked from website, the page has a mechanism to navigate to particular page through "contents" section. Alternatively, there is a mechanism to navigate page by page to avoid page break through "Pages" within contents section. In addition, the page has option to "Add Bookmark" and update the list of bookmarks under the section "Bookmarks" within contents:

DOI: 10.1201/9781003299431-14

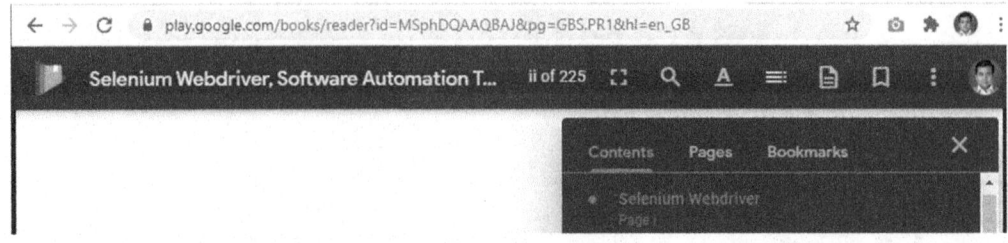

Picture: Image of Google Play display of sample ebook.

In addition to the features, there is an option to zoom the pages up to 200%, which has helped CBK to zoom the page to 200% to start reading the content slowly:

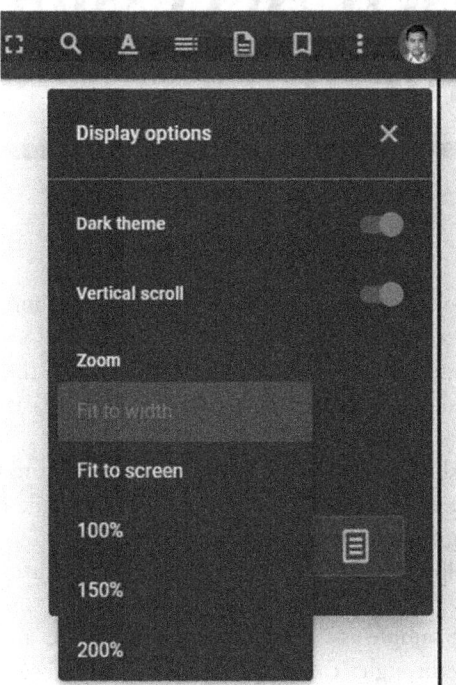

Picture: Features within Google Play display of ebook.

In addition to all these features, CBK liked the destination markers across the book on contents section.

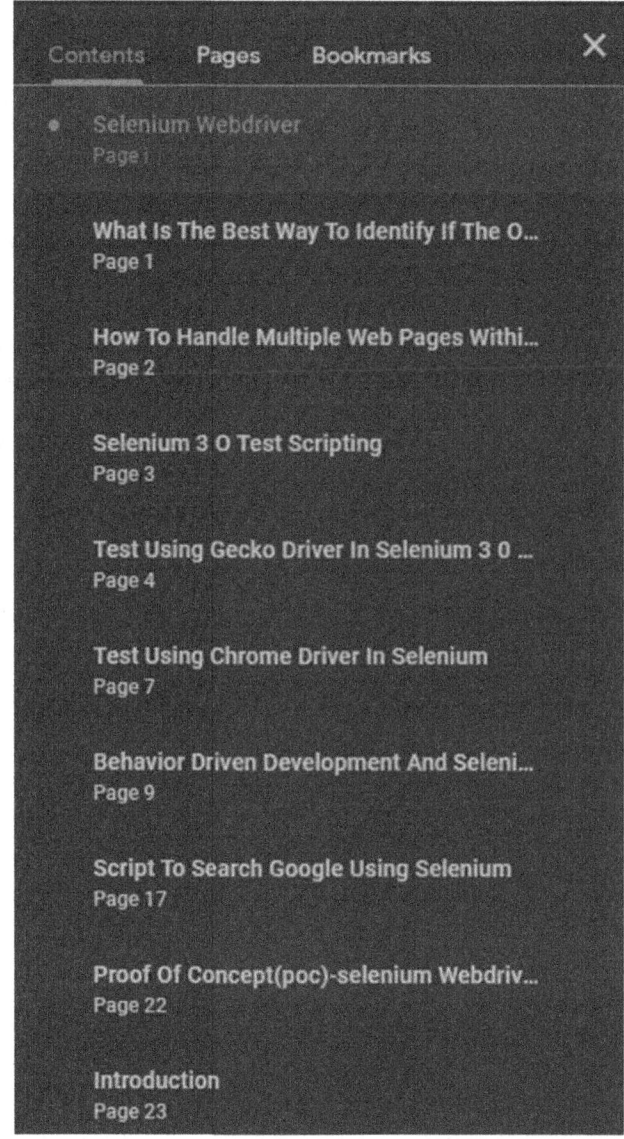

Picture: Image displaying different pages of the ebook from "Selenium Webdriver" through Google Play.

After having this checked in CBK, he got an idea on what to expect in his scope of testing as below:

- Every digital version of ebook to match the pages in line with printed book on each chapter.
- If the digital version of the eBook does not have a print version as alternative, it has to have clear pagination details to help user navigate between the pages and sections.

Naren and CBK started testing their terms and conditions and found their first defect on their features available to navigate to each page and sections:

Picture: Page break from ebook part of Google Play free sample.

There was no feature made available to look at the contents of the eBook and the user has to go to each page to understand what content has been provided where as the printed copy of the book has "Table of contents," which is missing in the digital version.

Naren includes tests related to page-break-before, page-break-after, and page-break-inside to verify when PDF versions and ebooks need testing part of websites.[3]

Both CBK and Naren had a discussion with Mark to understand what options they are left with to improve the page break experience and Mark explained some tricks around html properties.

Updating page list navigation with <nav role="ebook-pagelist"> would help announcing it through screen reader and, similarly, designations can be marked with a span property as <span id="page1"> and both these two types of updates would help improve page break experience[4].

Now Naren went back to update his test cases and Mark worked toward the page break feature improvements for better accessibility experience.

We learnt about techniques involved in testing paged media in this chapter and it is important to understand what tests to undertake when websites are developed as "single page applications" in the next chapter.

Notes

1. Title: Page Break Locators. (Accessed 12 December 2021). Retrieved from https://www.w3.org/WAI/WCAG22/Understanding/page-break-navigation.html#dfn-page-break-locators
2. Title: Selenium Webdriver-Software Automation Testing Secrets Revealed. (Accessed 12 December 2021). Retrieved from https://play.google.com/store/books/details?id=MSphDQAAQBAJ&rdid=book-MSphDQAAQBAJ&rdot=1
3. Title: Paged Media. (Accessed 12 December 2021). Retrieved from https://www.w3.org/TR/CSS22/page.html
4. Thanks to Luke McGrath on his blog: Web Accessibility for Developers, Title: Page Break Navigation (2.4.13 – Level A). (Accessed 13 December 2021). Retrieved from https://www.wuhcag.com/page-break-navigation/

Chapter 14

Single Page Application-based Accessibility Development

Single Page Applications (SPA) are the future of web development and traditionally multi-page websites that cause delays in loading entire pages through browsers since page rendering time delay, reload time, and refresh time. But these full page reload are avoided by part of the page load through JSON format data in single page application and it gets extended when user scroll down to see the page further in which further JSON data are shared to display the remaining part of the page. Initial server call returns HTML page but consecutive calls get JSON-based data to load that particular part of the page to avoid wastage of unnecessary data transmission.

On a flip side, it will be extremely difficult for screen readers (text-to-speech assistive technology applications commonly used by differently abled users) to understand when the page reloaded with additional set of data. For example, pressing INSERT+F7 to load "Elements List" would not show the complete list of links in the page since the page itself is partially loaded.

Examples: React-based developments like Facebook, Gmail website, LinkedIn feeds, etc.

When this question of SPA's level of accessibility adherence in Linkedin was asked, it got mixed answers as below:

It clearly proves that the SPA may provide good accessibility features but it needs a proper accessibility testing cycle to test and learn any challenges while accessing through assistive technologies, such as screen readers.

When Naren found that couple of new projects are getting developed using SPA model, he thought to include tests specific to SPA to find defects early in life cycle. Let us look at some of the examples from the code while launching SPA-based websites and technical limitations in this chapter.

Example 1—Live newsfeed not announcing the latest display of news items or posts:

LinkedIn with NVDA screen reader tries loading the newsfeeds of LinkedIn and tries to access it from NVDA and it can easily be determined if latest newsfeed is reflected or not reflected in screen reader announcements.

Example 2—Clear announcement of newly displayed items when user scroll down:

Naren tried to access Shackleton case study[1] from Harvard Business School Online using NVDA screen reader here:

DOI: 10.1201/9781003299431-15

NARAYANAN PALANI (He/Him)
Engineering Leadership Chapter Lead Chief QA …
2d ·

#questionnaire of the day

How Single Page Applications (SPA) help users
with disabilities generally-will they provide better
#Accessibility? …see more

You can see how people vote. Learn more

SPA provide best accessibility	75%
Most Complex in Text-To-Speech	0%
NotUseful Even if Aria Updated	0%
Can't comment until tested	25%

Picture: Linkedin survey of Narayanan Palani on SPA.

He noticed that every section is displayed by a "next" button click is being announced clearly: Important benefit about accessibility implementation in this website:

When user scrolls down to next sections on the same page, elements list of screen reader (which gets opened by pressing INSERT+F7 in NVDA screen reader) is automatically updated with new section fields when navigating between the radio buttons:

It means that user now know that there is a video which has several options to choose like rewind, faster, and slower, etc.

Key Recommendations

When SPAs are tested, "navigation using keyboard" needs a complete testing. Naren had a doubt of focus order on SPA pages and he was discussing with CBK on how to deal with dynamic loaded contents due to one of the key challenge. When traditional pages are reloaded, the focus moved to top of the page and announce page title and complete page elements to get the items read from top to bottom to understand all the available items. But it is not the case with dynamic loaded contents since if user is on a dropdown and choses a particular value and that needs additional information to be loaded on the page dynamically, it gets loaded on the page but the focus remains on the same dropdown where the user was originally focused. Hence getting newly loaded items to announce the part of screen reader is essential in this part of accessibility testing specific to SPA pages.

NVDA Speech Viewer

button collapsed   graphic   NARAYANAN PALANI
button collapsed   Me
button collapsed   Work
link   Advertise   out of list
Banner advertisement   frame   heading   level 5   link   The UCL MBA — Now Online -
link   An online MBA programme for professionals with 5+ years of experience.
Banner advertisement   frame   heading   level 5   link   The UCL MBA — Now Online -
link   An online MBA programme for professionals with 5+ years of experience.
link   Advertise   out of list
button collapsed   Work
button collapsed   graphic   NARAYANAN PALANI
NVDA Speech Viewer
Show Speech Viewer on Startup   check box   checked   Alt+s
NVDA Speech Viewer
Review
Ribbon Display Options Show or hide the Ribbon to maximize space.
Type to search and use the up and down arrows keys to navigate Tell Me (Alt+Q)
Just start typing here to bring features to your fingertips and get help.
Minimize Moves the window out of the way
(1) Feed | LinkedIn - Google Chrome
(1) Feed | LinkedIn   document
button collapsed   graphic   NARAYANAN PALANI
chart
Play

☑ Show Speech Viewer on Startup

Picture: Image of NVDA Speech Viewer not reading the latest newsfeeds of LinkedIn posts.

Test Case Template

John Sweet's Accessibility in Single Page Apps (Part 1[2] and 2[3]) are some of the best websites to refer with code examples on accessibility best practices and it is recommended to readers to continue exploring the coverage improvement of accessibility tests based on latest single page application developments.

We learnt about latest development of websites on SPA model and how to test them with different techniques. The next step is to learn on how to cover a test for redundant entry on different forms and user input sections on websites.

NVDA Speech Viewer

clickable banner landmark link Harvard Business School Online - Lessons
main landmark A 35 MINUTE INTERACTIVE LESSON WITH PROF.
Minimize
Shackleton's Endurance Expedition Part I – Harvard Business School Online – Lessons - Google Chrome
Shackleton's Endurance Expedition Part I – Harvard Business School Online – Lessons
document
clickable banner landmark link Harvard Business School Online - Lessons
Next section
button
link Harvard Business School Online - Lessons
main landmark Section 2 of 11 region Section 2 of 11 You're forming a new team
to undertake a high stakes venture. What would you prioritize when hiring? heading
level 2 grouping Select the attribute you would prioritize when hiring out of
grouping Submit button unavailable Next section button
Next section
Next section button
Select the attribute you would prioritize when hiring grouping
list
Technical Skills radio button checked 1 of 6
Submit button
Shackleton's Endurance Expedition Part I – Harvard Business School Online – Lessons
document
clickable main landmark Section 2 of 11 region Responses display type, section 3
navigation landmark list with 2 items Display chart view toggle button pressed
FolderView
Interactive chart
FolderView

☑ Show Speech Viewer on Startup

Picture: NVDA Speech Viewer announcing clear list of items from the case study.

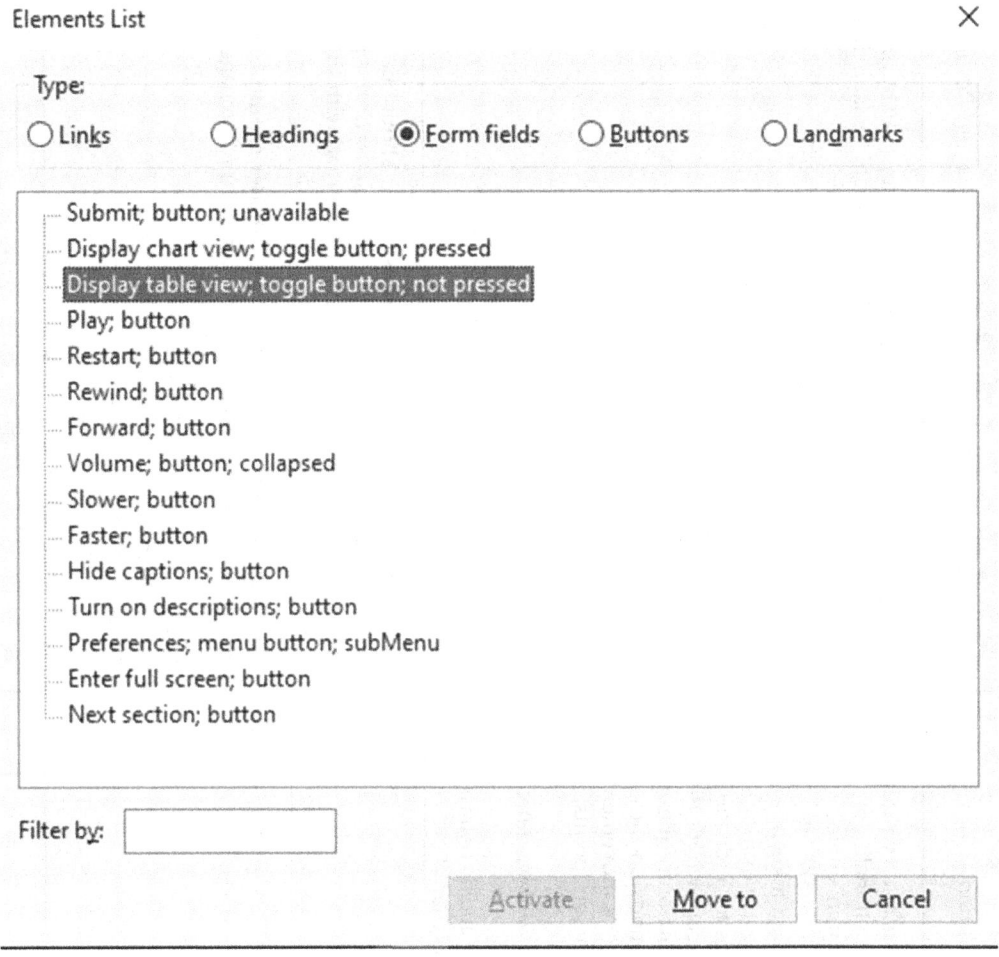

Picture: NVDA Screen Reader's element list.

*Test Name	Description	Step Name	Step Description	Step Expected Results
WCAG_2.1.1_KeyboardAccessible_SinglePageApplication	This test case has been written to verify all functionality of the content within single page applications (SPA) is operable through a keyboard interface without requiring specific timings for individual keystrokes, except where the underlying function requires input that depends on the path of the user's movement and not just the endpoints. Refer to the WCAG Guidelines:https://www.w3.org/TR/UNDERSTANDING-WCAG20/visual-audio-contrast-text-presentation.html	Step 1	Launch NVDA Screen Reader from Windows Operating System and enable audio to listen to the screen reader. Note:-Right click on NVDA, choose Tools and select Speech Viewer. Alternatively, Launch JAWS screen reader.	Screen reader (NVDA or JAWS) should be launched successfully.
		Step 2	Launch the browser and enter the URL of the website to test.	Website URL should be read out and display of the page should be read with title and other details.
		Step 3	Press Tab from keyboard and navigate inside the website; use down/up/left/right arrow keys to navigate to the images available in the pageNote: avoid using mouse from this step; keyboard usage is recommended	Screen reader should read contents from the page clearly.

Step 4	Use the keyboard shortcuts in the attachment (comments column) and perform testing on the website using keyboard only. Additional References:JAWS Screen Reader:Use the keyboard shortcuts mentioned in the website below and test the website:https://webaim.org/resources/shortcuts/jawsNVDA Screen Reader:https://dequeuniversity.com/screenreaders/nvda-keyboard-shortcuts	Keyboard shortcuts should announce the respective section of the web page.Note:If there are multiple Tables, pressing T should result in going to next table. Similarly use the keyboard shortcuts to navigate in table cells: Ctrl + Alt + down arrow or up arrow or left arrow or right arrow.
Step 5	Use INSERT+F7 from NVDA screen reader to launch Elements List when the SPA page is loaded and try to navigate between radio button options between links, headings, etc.	Available fields/elements from SPA should be listed in the elements list.
Step 6	Try to scroll down or expand the sections to dynamically load the content part of SPA and make sure the change the radio buttons to verify links, headings, landmarks, form fiels within elements list are updated with latest displayed content.	Latest available fields/elements should be listed as part of elements list.

Notes

1. Title: Shackleton's Endurance Expedition. Retrieved from https://lessons.online.hbs.edu/shackleton/
2. Title: Accessibility in Single Page Apps (Part 1). Retrieved from https://johnsweetaccessibility.com/2020/05/accessibility-in-spas-part-1/
3. Title: Accessibility in Single Page Apps (Part 2). Retrieved from https://johnsweetaccessibility.com/2020/05/accessibility-in-spas-part-2/

Chapter 15

Website Redundant Entry-based Accessibility Development

Yamini received a strange defect from her production support team that their customers were unable to auto-populate the flight passenger details when they change the flight timings during ticket purchase. She did not understand why such defect is related to accessibility. Later while reading about latest WCAG 2.2 guidelines, she learnt about "Redundant Entry" guidelines.[1]

She now knows that user already entered their details the first time, revisiting the same page, it should allow the user to either select the previously selected data or automatically populate as long as the passenger details need not change. But this defect particularly comes into picture when a user is trying to change the flight details without affecting passenger details.

On a contrary, when this defect was taken to Mark, he suggested that fields such as password should not be supposed to be auto-filled. Hence Yamini got this tagged as severity 2 defect to get this fixed for every form fields except security related fields, such as password fields.

After speaking to Yamini and Mark, Naren knew that it is one of the important tests to write to verify redundant entries in different scenarios when amendments being made in user inputs of the websites.

Especially in case of users with mental fatigue or memory-related disabilities, it will be a difficult and exhausting experience for them when re-entering the values for the fields if there is need to repeat the action for any small amendments. Hence every user input forms or input fields need a consideration for this accessibility guideline WCAG SC 3.3.8 to adhere to Level A guidelines.

We learnt the need for redundant entry tests to verify the latest guidelines on WCAG 3.3.8 in this chapter and it is important to learn about how to get drag and drop functionalities adhered to accessibility guidelines—let us learn these techniques in the next chapter.

Note

1. Title: Success Criterian 3.3.8 Redundant Entry. Retrieved from https://www.w3.org/TR/WCAG22/#redundant-entry

Chapter 16

Website Drag and Drop Functionality-based Accessibility Development

Claire received a recent update from their business analyst Juliet Sullivan that they are looking for options to introduce drag and drop functionalities in the project for a complete list of work items in grocery online sales portfolio. She ringed Nicholas, their accessibility consultant to explain the situation and he agreed to get it tested with initial developed page in first instance to provide feedback.

But the real challenge was that Mark, the front-end engineer, had no idea on what kind of accessibility features are available first in place to get it read to users through screen readers.

"Mark, if you are a front-end developer, you should know what are the defects possible in drag and drop first," said Nicholas.

Nicholas has set a workshop between CBK, Naren, Mark, Sandhya, and himself as it is one of the nice options to explore nice code examples.

While showing examples from w3schools website in the workshop, Nicholas requested CBK to test the website example with drag and drop feature from w3school using NVDA screen reader on a Chrome browser:

https://www.w3schools.com/html/html5_draganddrop.asp

While testing this feature, CBK could not continue to drag the image to right hand side rectangle with keyboard alone. He needed a mouse but he did not know where the mouse is dragging the image when using one since he is 70% vision impaired.

But Mark argued that drag and drop is traditionally a widely used feature in many websites and why this defect is coming on his way? CBK hunted down the key WCAG guideline and shared to Mark:

"Success Criterion 2.5.7 Dragging Movements (Level AA): All functionality that uses a dragging movement for operation can be achieved by a single pointer without dragging, unless dragging is essential." Source[1]

DOI: 10.1201/9781003299431-17

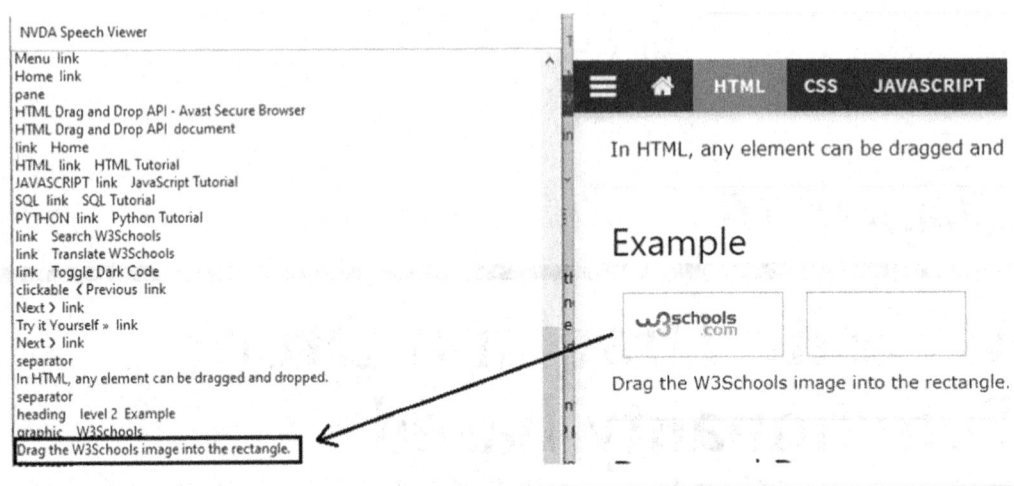

Picture: NVDA Speech Viewer announcing about drag feature of a website.

After reading this WCAG guideline, all were convinced that the drag and drop solution provided conventionally by dragging an item from source to drop it to destination is no longer an accessibility friendly feature and the SRF website ought to get it right since the whole SRF group is adhered to WCAG Level AA (it means that they should not leak any A and AA level defects but AAA is optional). Hence CBK testing has been abrupted without completing the action.

Thus the session became more interesting and Nicholas requested CBK to test another website. This time salesforce[2] GitHub website with the best example of drag and drop functionality taken into consideration to evaluate against the accessibility guidelines.

When CBK tested the feature, he not only completed the drag and drop option but also explained on how easy it was for him to perform it:

Advantages:

- Each section that needs to drag has been provided as a link.
- Each target to drop has been provided as a menu item within the cell, hence pressing keyboard TAB helped him navigate to menu items to choose right destination to drop the item.

Now Mark has requested Sandhya to re-align their UX Design documents to match the needs of better accessibility as per the success criterion 2.5.7.

Lessons Learnt:
Even though screen readers read the elements from source of the drag and drop functionalities, it doesn't mean users with disabilities (who are mainly with keyboards and not equipped with mouse/mice) may not drag the items correctly to drop them to destination. Hence adding links and menu items helps in making the drag and drop feature with the best accessible user interaction.

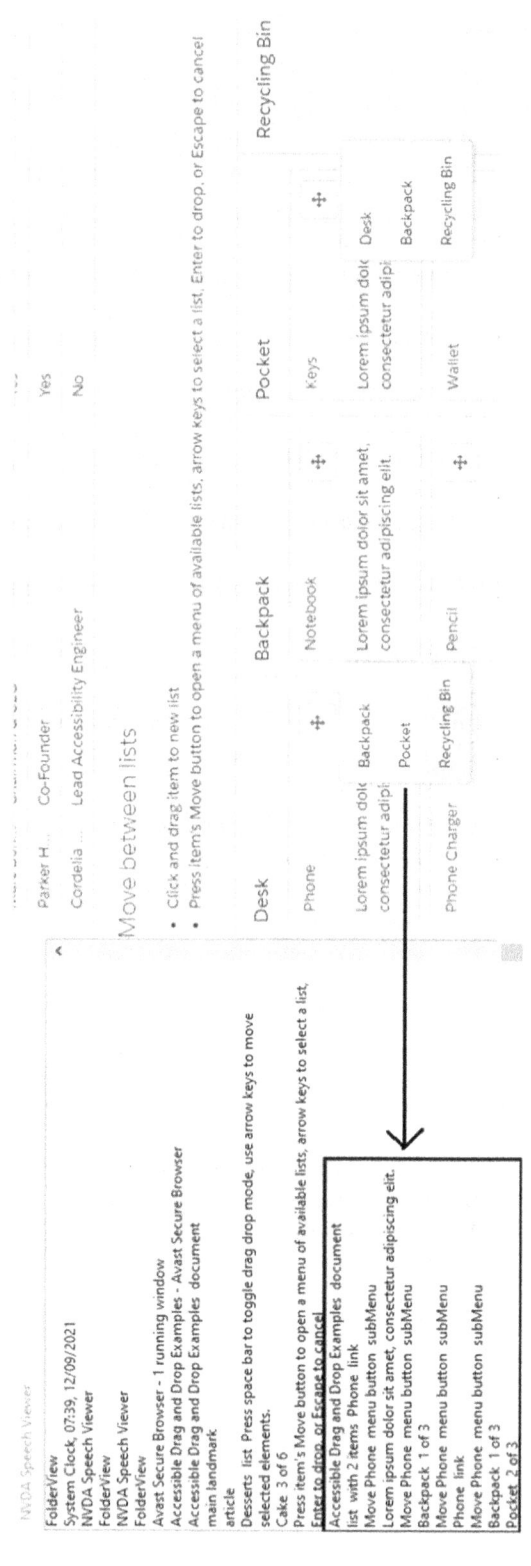

Picture: NVDA Speech Viewer announcing about the drag and drop feature.

Screen Reader Defects

Naren was testing a web component built by Mark with accessibility properties such as aria-label, title, and other necessary attributes to give better accessibility to each objects being displayed on the User Interface. As a first hand test, Mark scanned the page with Axe chrome extension and he did not find any violations related to accessibility, hence he was happy to let Naren testing the page with screen reader.

In the beginning, Naren chose JAWS and Internet Explorer browser to run tests and they were all announcing as expected. But he restarted the same tests with NVDA screen reader but did not find some announcements of few objects, which was originally read earlier in JAWS tests. To the surprise of front End engineer, Naren logged this as a defect and requested him to review.

Solution:
After CBK and Mark reviewed the defect pertaining to NVDA, they understood that aria properties are appropriate, which was proven while testing in JAWS screen reader as an example. Hence they recommended Naren to post the defect in NVDA's screen reader list of defects external since it is not the problem of their application but the problem could be with screen reader itself.

When any issues are identified in NVDA Screen reader[3] itself, it is worth raising them over an issue ticket.

Similarly JAWS screen reader[4] provided a dedicated support website to help customers with any issues.

We have been learning about different website-based features to test against accessibility guidelines so far such as page title, heading, landmark, drag, and drop. Now it is time to learn about how pictures can be handled in websites since visually impaired users are one of the major impacted user group when images and pictures are provided in websites to represent information. Let us learn some key concepts used in testing the images in the last part (of first half of the book)—mainly from Yamini, our SME on web accessibility.

Notes

1. Title: Understanding Success Criterion 2.5.7: Dragging Movements. Retrieved from https://www.w3.org/WAI/WCAG22/Understanding/dragging-movements
2. Title: D&D INTERACTION PATTERNS. Retrieved from https://salesforce-ux.github.io/dnd-a11y-patterns/#/?_k=ae7cj9
3. Title: NVDA screen reader problems while reading code word by word in Microsoft visual studio code editor. Retrieved from https://github.com/nvaccess/nvda/issues/7605
4. Title: Technical Support-Freedom Scientific. Retrieved from https://support.freedomscientific.com/support

Chapter 17

Website Images-based Accessibility Development

Problem Statement

After testing several project releases for the SRF group of websites in the first major UI migration uplift, Naren and CBK were extremely exhausted since the projects are mostly reactive to the number of defects they find in accessibility and not finding the way out to prevent the defects in any possible ways.

At this stage, Claire reviewed the complete list of defects and realized that they are lacking skills on preventing accessibility defects, hence she recruited Yamini who is an accessibility consultant made to work purely as an Accessibility Waiver Board to sign off accessibility defects and helps in introducing accessibility earlier in product life cycle.

After joined to the organization, Yamini spoke to key QEs and realized that there were number of testing practices missing.

They are:

- Testing the images before UI gets developed.
- Testing the UI design templates against minimum color contrast requirements of WCAG.

Images Testing Basics

"A text alternative (in any possible wordings) is required for every non-text element," Yamini told this to the entire QE team across the SRF group.

Users with vision impairment do not have direct access to pictures. They listen to their screen readers read the image's alternate text, which was provided by the developer or content producer or by design engineers. The text is translated from text to speech screen readers that vision blind users can feel with their ears in the case of vision blind users with partial vision loss.

Depending on whether the image is presented in the <img> element, via Scalable Vector Graphics (SVG) markup, via the HTML 5 <canvas> element, or via another way, different

DOI: 10.1201/9781003299431-18

strategies for providing alternative text are used. However, the premise remains the same: the alternative text must be meaningful and act as an appropriate replacement for the image in a form that is understandable to blind users.

Alternative representations are frequently required for other types of content as well, such as:

■ Graphics (which requires captions, a transcript, and which may require audio descriptions)
■ Sound (which requires a transcript, at a minimum)
■ Add-ons (e.g., Silverlight and Flash, which require effective use of their respective accessibility APIs)
■ Paperwork (e.g., Word, PowerPoint, PDF, etc., which also require effective use of their respective APIs)

Because HTML usually offers the greatest potential for accessibility across the widest range of devices, it's often desirable to build an HTML-based alternate version for non-HTML material.

Discussion with Mark, the front-end engineer, resulted in a debate between himself and Yamini on which aria attribute must be used for images since mark was liking to use aria-label for every image but Yamini mentioned a number of options, including title, alt, as well as aria-labelledby (in addition to aria-label). While Mark challenged Yamini on why he needs to use different options for one image, she explained that it is not necessary to add all four properties to all images but carefully select them on the basis of need. She also went on to setup a series of training sessions to engineers across the SRF organization to learn on different techniques while verifying images on the website against accessibility guidelines. The next couple of pages are basically extract from her key lessons.

Screen Readers Understand Attribute in a Particular Priority on their Inbuilt Code

Even though each screen reader is built based on different programming repositories and different programming languages, every <img> Element's Calculation Algorithm for Accessible Name from Screen Reader works in this way generally:

In most circumstances, the alt attribute is the conventional (recommended) method, but there are additional options:

■ aria-labelledby: If an aria-labelledby property exists, the text it belongs to will assume control over all other values.
■ aria-label: All other values will be overridden by the aria-label text (if aria-labelledby is not specified).
■ Alt: This is the standard method of giving alternative text (note that if either an aria-labelledby or an aria-label property is present, the alt text will not be read at all).
■ Title: If no other option is available, screen readers will read the title attribute text as a last alternative.

Mark is yet to get convinced and he searched on WCAG websites and landed on to some nice examples[2] and code references.[3]

Best Practices for Alternative Text

After speaking to Yamini, Sandhya (Designer) had questions on ways to make images accessible in a variety of situations, including instructive, decorative, sophisticated, and animated images.

Yamini setup an session exclusively for "lternative text" and she explained on what is good:

- Discernible (the Alternative text can be accessed by screen reader)
- Concise (the alternative text should not or recommended not to exceed 150 characters, and ideally should be considerably shorter)
- Meaningful (the alternative text appropriately expresses the purpose of the image or the author's objective in utilizing the image)
- Simple (the alternative texts should not use jargons and it is recommended to use simple words)

If the image is just decorative or superfluous, it's better to hide it from screen readers (e.g., using attributes such as "alt")[4].

While implementing on web UI, Sandhya wanted the same properties to be used in internal word documentations that represent content copy with same images and she spoke to Mark on this and realized that it won't work with Word documents or PowerPoint slides, surprisingly.

If the image reveals a lot of crucial information, it will need to be accompanied by a lengthy supplementary description such as this:

Image:

Picture: Work from home setup[5].

Alternative Text: Image representing laptop, monitor, keyboard, mobile phone, mouse, earphone along with a table lamp in a working from home setup.

Now Sandhya knows on what to get as a text alternative and she is thinking to engage both business analyst Juliet and quality engineer Naren to draft these texts while her design and images getting ready. The objective is to get the text alternative "copy tested" hence Yamini's first goal of shift left accessibility has been initiated at this point.

Lessons Learnt: If you don't perform accessibility testing at the design and images level, you are loosing opportunities and time when defects are found in development and testing phase. As a famous quote of GK Chesterton states, "The only way of catching a train I ever discovered is to miss the train before." Since Naren and CBK already missed the train in their first few releases of product development, they learnt it by now. Hence designer works with BA/QE on test alternative and front-end engineer started documenting alt properties with those reviewed texts before UI development kickstarts in the feature development.

Image that is Not of Any Use Without Alternate text

Naren started testing new SRF group releases with their images provisioned by Sandhya (Designer) for the development work. While testing the images, he checked with Mark on what was the planned html5 semantic elements planned to get used for first set of images since Mark also started developing the properties table in parallel with Sandhya.

Naren found that one of the images has no discernible alt text. Most screen readers would read the image file name—in an attempt to read something so it would sound like this "graphic car dot JPG.", which is not very helpful in this instance.

Image: Vintage Car[6].

Code:

```
<img src="car.jpg" width="686" height="518">
```

Informative Images and New Necessity

"Alternative text must be programmatically identifiable for images that transmit content. Naren wrote a detailed defect to get image properties updated.

Images cannot be read or interpreted directly by screen readers. They are only able to read the author's alternate text. Authors must use the alt attribute on the img element to give a programmatically identifiable text alternative for an image.

First Hot Fix: Image with Words That Aren't Appropriate in the Alt

Mark got a quick hot fix and requested QE to test it immediately. Naren found that the image includes the words "A photo of" in the alt text. Screen readers would say, "Graphic, A photo of an orange color antique car". He thought it is a clear defect again hence he did not close the defect at all and left it re-opened.

Code:

```
<img src="antiquecar.jpg" width="686" height="518" alt="A photo of an orange color antique car">
```

Reason:

Words that Identify the Element as a Visual or Image SHOULD NOT be Included in the Alternative Text.

In most circumstances, inserting "image of" or "graphic of" or "picture of" in the alternative text for an img is superfluous because screen readers announce "image" or "graphic" as they read the alternative text for an img. Those words should only be included in the alternative text if it is critical to show that an image is a photograph or an illustration.

The Alternate Text for Informational Photos SHOULD be kept to a Minimum (No More than About 150 Characters)

Although there is no technical or policy limit on the length of alt text, it is less useful than plain text for various reasons:

- If a screen reader user pauses in the middle of reading alt text, they will not be able to resume where they left off.
- Users with screen readers are unable to navigate the content (e.g. by word, character, etc.).
- Some older screen readers don't read the alt text in it's entirety.

Not required to go into full detail about every aspect of the image. That would be far too much information, and no one would want to sit through such a lengthy description. They say that a picture is worth a thousand words, but alt text should not even come close to that. The alt attribute was designed to be used for short alternative text. In some ways, the suggestion to be succinct appears to contradict the advice to be descriptive. It's tough to be both concise and descriptive at the same time. In fact, with complicated visuals, it can be nearly impossible. It's usually rather simple to be both quick and informative with most photographs.

Post Fix no.2- Image with Easily Recognized Alt Text from Mark

Mark fixed once again and this time this image has discernible alt text. Screen readers would say, "Graphic, A Ford model antique Car."
Code:

```
<img src="Ford car.jpg" width="686" height="518" alt="A Ford model antique Car">
```

Now Naren closed the defect and updated the comment section in JIRA that the image section of the website is now adhering to WCAG guidelines "Understanding Success Criterion 1.1.1: Non-text Content."

But looking at the defect, Yamini thought she would love to give a session to engineering audiences on what it means as alternative text and how important it is. Since it is the only mode of instruction for users with vision loss since images are irrelevant to them in case of 100% vision blindness.

So she created an internal channel of chat group to share some more insights with engineers who are part of the feature team and start sharing her daily insights to whole team in a easiest way.

Useful Guidelines for Alternative Texts

Alternative text for instructive images MUST be relevant (exactly communicating the image's purpose and the author's aim in a way that is useful to people who cannot see it).

The goal of alt text is to give users with vision blindness a description of the image. If the image cannot be seen, the alt text must provide a suitable substitute. The alternative text should properly represent the image's function so that the user understands why the image is present and what it represents as quickly as possible. This module will go through many methods to alternative text depending on how an image is utilized, but bear in mind that alternative text should be used to clearly explain the image's goal, purpose, and meaning in a way that acts as a true replacement for the image.

It's a good idea to think about the following questions while determining what to include in the alternative:

■ What is the purpose of this non-textual content?
■ What kind of data is it displaying?
■ What function does it serve?
■ What words would I use to convey the same information if I couldn't use the non-text content?

Meaningful Alternative Texts

Best Example: Meaningful General-Purpose Alt Text for an Informative Image

The alt text for the photograph describes the situation displayed. This alt text is fine in general, however it might not be appropriate for a more specific application of the same image.

Picture: Nature Scenery of a Tree[7].

Code:

```
<img src="nature.jpg" width="700" height="466" alt="Its nature's scenery with blue and green background along with a tree">
```

Best Example: Alternative Text for an Image's Specialized Purpose

The Developer's goal with this image is to talk about photographic exposure techniques and how exposing for one part of the scene causes another part of the scene to be underexposed. It would be impolite to just describe the contents of the image. The alt text should explain why the author chose to include the image. The aim and author's objective in this context should be described in the alt text, which is not the same as a general explanation of what is in the image.

Code:

```
<img src="nature.jpg" width="700" height="466" alt="The camera was set to properly expose the greenery in this scene, resulting in greenery of the land and tree in the foreground, and blue sky">
```

Best Example: Logo of Informative Images

The alt text explains the image's purpose, which is to identify the brand rather than to describe its appearance.

Picture: NP Logo of Narayanan Palani[8].

Code:

```
<img src="np.png" alt="narayanan palani logo" width="245" height="158>
```

It may be permissible to refer to this image as a logo in some instances. For example, the alt text may say alt="np logo." Identifying the brand, on the other hand, is usually sufficient. It all depends on the message the author is trying to convey.

Bad Example (Not Recommended): Image with No Useful Alt Text

This image has alt text that does not adequately describe the image. "An ink," it states, omitting the crucial information supplied by the image's text: "Danger."

Picture: Image of Danger Ink Print on Floor[9].

Code:

```
<img src="Danger.png" width="640" height="452" alt="An ink">
```

Bad Example (Not Recommended): Empty Alt Text on an Informative Image

Because the alt text for this image is blank, screen readers will ignore it completely, and viewers will be unaware that the image exists at all. On purely ornamental or redundant photos, empty alt text is fine, but it is not permitted on informative images.

Code:

```
<img src="danger.png" width="640" height="452" alt="">
```

Informative Image Example

Best Example: Concise Alt Text: Informative Image

The alt text succinctly summarizes the image's purpose.

Picture: Image of Zebra Herd[10].

Code:

```
<img src="herdofZebra.png" width="600" alt="A herd of Zebra walking alongside a stream in the Tarangire National park">
```

Bad Example (Not Recommended): Image with Excessive Alt Text on *herdofZebra.png*

This image has a long alt text that should be placed on its own and read in conjunction with shorter alt text.

```
<img src="herdofzebra.png" width="600" alt="In this photograph, few Zebras are walking on dry land next to a stream of water. In the foreground, down in the bottom right corner, is a part of a bush. The reflection of the herd of elephants can be seen in the water Behind the Zebras are thickets that stretch for miles and miles. The thickets then give way to the mountains set in the background.">
```

Decorative or Redundant Images

Null Alternative Text (alt=""), ARIA Role="Presentation," or CSS Backgrounds Must Be Used for Images that do not Provide Content, are Decorative, or are Redundant to Content that is Already Expressed in Text

For images that do not convey information or do not require alternative text since the image is described in the page content, use "null" alt attributes (using att).

Some developers make the mistake of dropping the alt attribute entirely from images that they believe do not require it. This is inconvenient for assistive technology users since the source attribute (i.e., file name) is frequently viewed as the alternative text by the screen reader. Use the alt="blank alternative text" attribute to inform assistive technology to ignore an image.

Best Example: Redundant Image with Null Alt Text

Both the link text and the image are placed within the anchor tag in this example. Because the image adds no more information and is solely decorative, the alt text is left blank (alt=" ").

```
<a href="https://engineers-hub.teachable.com">
<img src="board-icon.png" width="24" height="29" alt=" ">
Board Exam
</a>
```

Bad Example (Not Recommended) : Image with Redundant Alt Text that Duplicates Adjacent Text

The anchor tag contains the link text as well as the image in this example. Because the image's alt text is the same as the link's, a screen reader will read "link Board Exam." The alt text should be left blank in situations like this, where the image adds no extra information (is indeed decorative) (alt).

```
<a href="https://engineers-hub.teachable.com">
<img src="board-icon.png" width="24" height="29" alt="Board Exam">
Board Exam
</a>
```

Actionable Image (Buttons, Links, Controls)

Alternative text is required for any actionable images (e.g., links, buttons, and controls).

Make sure that the alternative text for actionable graphics conveys the destination, purpose, function, or action in detail. Screen readers will notify that the image is a "link graphic" before presenting the alt text, therefore don't put "link to" in the alt text.

"If non-text content is a control or accepts user input, it has a name that explains its purpose," according to WCAG 2.1-1.1.1. When images are used as controls, the alternative text should describe the control's action rather than the image itself.

Best Example: The Alt Text on the Image used as a Link is of Good Help

The image below is a blue circle with an icon of a white in the middle of it. You could describe it in detail like that, but it would be more appropriate in a case like this to simply say what the image does, which is link to the My Computer. The most appropriate alt text is simply "My computer".

```
<a href="#">
<img src="My computer.png" alt="My computer Page" width="113">
</a>
```

Bad Example (Not Recommended): Link used in Image Lacks Alt Text

This example uses the same blue circle with a white to connect to the My Computer, but the image lacks alt text.

```
<a href="#">
<img src="my computer.png" width="113" height="113">
</a>
```

Recommendation: For Actionable Pictures such as "Submit Here" Buttons, the Alternative Text MUST be Meaningful (Accurately Conveying the Purpose or Result of the Action)

It is critical that the alternative text for actionable images describes the image's purpose or functionality. For example, the alternative text for a link picture will describe the link destination rather than the image's shape or other visual qualities. The alternate wording for a button image will convey the button's functionality (e.g., a "Submit" button or "Enroll" button).

Words that Identify the Element as a Link, Graphic, or Picture SHOULD NOT be Included in the Alternative Text

When reading the alternative text for an image, screen readers say "image" or "graphic," and when the image is inside an anchor tag, they say "link." As a result, words like "link to," "picture of," and "graphic of" are redundant in the alternative text. The link's destination or action should be described in the alternative text.

Bad Example (Not Recommended): Inappropriate Words in the Image's Alt

This image includes the words "A link to" in the alt text. Screen readers would say, "Link, Graphic, A link to the My Computer page."
Code:

```
<a href="#">
<img src="My computer.png" width="113" alt="A link to the My computer page">
</a>
```

The Alternate Wording for Actionable Photos SHOULD be kept to a Minimum (No More than About 150 Characters)

There is no technical limit nor policy restriction on the length of alt text, but alt text is not as usable as regular text for several reasons according to me, Yamini continued:

- If a screen reader user pauses in the middle of reading alt text, they will not be able to resume where they left off.
- Users with screen readers are unable to navigate the content (e.g. by word, character, etc.).
- Some older screen readers don't read the alt text in its entirety.

Bad Example (Not Recommended): Longer than Needed Image Link with Alt Text

"Use this image link to go to the My computer page," states the alt text for this image link, however it would be better to simply offer the name of the page to which the link leads: "My computer".

```
<a href="#">
<img src="My computer.png" width="113" alt="Use this image link to go to My computer
page" >
</a>
```

Form Inputs Type="image"

Alternative text is required for form inputs with type="image."
You must utilize the alt attribute on the input element to make alternative text programmatically discernible for an input with type="image."

Best Example: With a Discernible Alt, Input Type="image"

The input button in the format of an image has alt text that explains the function of the image.

Picture: Image of Finish in a Button of website[11].

Code:

```
<input type="image" name="Finish" src="Finish-button.png" alt="Finish">
```

For Form Inputs with Type="Image," the Alternative Text Must Clearly Represent the Goal or Outcome of the Input Operation

Instead of describing the image's visual features, the alternative wording for an image input should describe the input's function.

Bad Example (Not Recommended): Without a Meaningful Alt, Type="image"

The input button in the form of an image has an alt attribute that describes the image rather than the purpose of the image.

```
<input type="image" name="Finish" src="Finish-button.png" alt="A red oval with shading
to look 3-d and white text.">
```

The Alternative Wording for Inputs with Type="image" SHOULD be kept to a Minimum (No More than About 140 to 150 Characters)

Note: Although there is no technical or policy limit on the length of alt text, it is not as useful as plain text for various reasons:

- If a screen reader user pauses in the middle of reading alt text, they will not be able to resume where they left off.
- Users with screen readers are unable to navigate the content (e.g., by word, character, etc.).
- Some older screen readers don't read the alt text in its entirety.

Bad Example (Not Recommended): Long Discernible Alt in input Type="image"

The input button in the format of an image has alt text that describes the function of the image, but it is still too long.

```
<input type="image" name="Finish" src="Finish-button.png" alt="Finish. Click this
button to Finish your Work.">
```

Animated Images

Any Prerecorded Video-Only Material that Starts Playing Automatically and Lasts Longer than 5 Seconds MUST Provide a Means to Pause, Stop, or Conceal It

People with certain types of cognitive disabilities, notably those with attention deficit disorders, may struggle with moving visual content. Moving information can be distracting, making it harder for users to focus on the web page's content. The 5-second threshold is long enough to catch people's attention, but not long enough to distract or prohibit them from using and interacting with the web content.

Flashing or Flickering Animated Visuals must not Exceed Three Times per Second

In persons with photosensitive epilepsy or other types of photosensitive seizure disorders, content that flashes or flickers more than three times per second may trigger a seizure. It's critical not to publish stuff that could cause your users to have seizures.

The Photosensitive Epilepsy Analysis Tool (PEAT) from the Trace Center is a free, downloadable resource for web content and software developers to identify seizure risks. This tool can be handy if you're unsure about a movie or animation that features flashing or rapid transitions between light and dark background colors.

Complex Picture or Visual Accessibility

Complex Visuals must have Both a Simple Alt Text Explanation and a Longer, More Clear Explanation

Even if you've successfully linked visual labels to visual data in a graph or chart, blind viewers will struggle to understand the images unless you include a clear text description. You might include the entire description in the alt text, however alt text should be kept to a minimum of about 150 characters. Although alt text can be much larger than 150 characters in length from a technological aspect, the convention is for alt text to be brief. You must use another approach if 150 characters or less are insufficient to describe an image.

A long description for an image can be provided in a number of ways.

1. Include the lengthy description within the HTML document itself.
2. Add a button that expands a collapsed region with the long description.
3. Include a button that launches a dialog with the long description.
4. Use normal link text to link to a long description on another page.
5. Use the long attribute to link to a long description on another page.

You must still give a concise alt text summarizing the image's principal purpose or content, regardless of the method you use.

Example

Picture: Graph Image with Statistics Representation of Tags[12].

For Sighted Users, the Full Description (or a Link or Button to Access the Long Description) SHOULD be Visible

For sighted users, some intricate visuals may be too complicated. As a result, having access to a detailed description of a complicated visual may be beneficial to some sighted people. If the description is provided via the Longdesc[13] attribute, sighted people will be unable to access the text-based information about the image.

Example:

Picture: Image of Laptop with Graphs and Bar Charts[14].

The Image SHOULD be Paired with the Long Description Programmatically

The longdesc element of the aria-describedby attributes makes the full alternative explanation for a complex image accessible to screen reader users. However, screen reader users can only utilize the longdesc approach. Screen reader users and non-screen reader users can both utilize other techniques, such as giving a link or embedding the description in the document.

```
<img src="tradingtrend.jpg" alt="Trading Trend" aria-describedby="description"> […] <p
id="description"> The trading trend of stock exchange with spot forward and swap rates
from the period 07Aug2021 00:00:00 to 08Aug2021 00:00:00 with green bars representing
trades which are spot, red bar which of swap with further trend analysis provided live </p>
```

Images of Text and Accessibility

If an Analogous Visual Display of the Information can be Generated Using Real Text, an Image MUST NOT Include Instructive Text

Except when the image is decorative in nature or the language in the image is crucial, utilize text instead of images of text wherever possible.

Best Example: Logo Text in Image

When the image is decorative in nature or the text in the image is essential, there is an exemption in WCAG that permits for the use of text in images. A company logo is a Best Example of this. When used as part of a logo, text in an image is OK. Remember to include all text that describes the logo's wording.

```
<img src="np_logo.png" width="165" height="59" alt="narayanan palani logo">
```

Picture: NP Logo of Narayanan Palani[15].

Recommendation: Despite the fact that logos frequently contain text, they are an exception to the rule that you should aim to utilize real text whenever possible.

Bad Example (Not Recommended): Nonessential Text in Image

Although adding alternative text for these photos would benefit screen readers, it may still be inaccessible to users of screen magnifiers or users who apply their own stylesheets to improve accessibility. Color inversion and text smoothing are common features of screen magnifiers that improve accessibility. When text is present in photos, such features will not operate, and the text will become illegible when magnified.

Picture: Image of Text with White Background sStating "You're not lost You're here"[16].

The typeface is viewable when magnified by screen magnifiers, although it is not as easy to read as genuine writing. Reading may be difficult for people with low eyesight.

Let us take an another example where a text provided as an image:

LOST

Picture: Image of Text with White Background Stating "lost"[17].

Recommendation: Unless the text is required (such as a logo), or the font, size, color, and background are adjustable, images should not incorporate useful text.

Screen reader users will be able to read text from photos that have a correct alternative description; however, persons with low eyesight will not be able to adjust the text in the images to read the text. Text in photographs can be kept as real text in a few ways, making it accessible to assistive technology users. Screen readers and low vision users can access and alter text in an image like SVG since it is treated as genuine text.

Best Example: Text Stylized with CSS

CSS can be used[18] to stylize text to match and replace text in images.

```
<div style="background: #aa061a; color: Black; width: 314px; max-height:101px; over-
flow:hidden; text-align:center; font-weight:bold;padding:39px 0;margin: auto; font-size:
50px; text-shadow: 5px 5px 5px #620915;"> LOST</div>
```

Best Example: Customizable Text in SVG Image

Imagine that a logo in SVG format has been provided with the text "Real text here" which will be rendered by a screen reader. Because the graphic is SVG, it can easily be scaled, which is beneficial to folks with low eyesight who may use screen resizing. Keep in mind that there must be enough contrast between the text and the background.

```
<svg width="150" height="150" role="img">
<rect width="150" height="150" fill="#0000FF" stroke="#000" stroke-width="1"/> <text
id="text" x="75" y="85" font-size="1em" text-anchor="middle" fill="#FFFFFF">#nplogo
</text>
</svg>
```

CSS Background Images

CSS Graphics that are Only Aesthetic or Superfluous in the HTML Content SHOULD NOT have a Text Alternative

Alternative text is not required for images that are just decorative or that are already detailed in the text next to the image. Because decorative graphics do not convey useful information to the user, no alternative text is required. If you supply the same information in an image's alt text as you do in the text content, a screen reader user will hear the information twice, potentially affecting the web page's usability

Best Example: Decorative Image Has No Text

Because the background image adds no information to the page, it does not require alt text.
    Refer the slack image provided in previous paragraph for the code below:

```
<div id="Writing"><p id="Slack">#Slack </p></div> #textContainer {
background-image:url("bg-abstract-wide.jpg");
background-repeat:no-repeat;
float:center;
padding:20px; }
#slack{
```

```
font: bold 30pt calibri; color:#FFFFFF;
text-align: center;}
```

Bad Example (Not Recommended): Decorative Image Does Not Need Text

Because the background image adds no value to the page, it should be left without alt text. Refer to the slack image provided earlier along with the code below to understand it better:

```
<div id="Writing">
<p id="Slack">#Slack</p>
<p class="visually-hidden">
A background image that is dark Black with light, Texture
</p>
</div>
```

Best Example: Decorative Background Image with No Alternative Text

This is a little background image that has been added with CSS. It is simply aesthetic, thus no equivalent text in the HTML is required.

Picture: Image of a Decorative Art of a Hindu God Lord Ganesha[19].

Code:

```
<span class="decorative_arts"></span>
```

Bad Example (Not Recommended): Background Image with Unnecessary Alternative Text

"decorative icon" is an unnecessary alternative text for this decorative graphic. Screen reader users will be irritated by written descriptions for decorative images, and it will detract from crucial content.

```
<span class="decorative_arts">
<span class="visually-hidden">decorative arts of Hindu God</span>
</span>
```

Alternative Text for Informative or Actionable CSS Graphics MUST be Present in the HTML Content as Programmatically Discernible Text

It's best to avoid including informational and actionable pictures in CSS wherever possible. You can, however, add alternate text to instructive and actionable CSS graphics if necessary. The examples below show how alternate text can be made available programmatically using the CSS clip method or the aria-label tag.

Best Example: Using aria-label, an Actionable (Connected) Backdrop Image with Alternative Text

Let us take an example of a link provided with aria-label to navigate to socialmedia a sample site of SRF Group:
Code:

```
<a    href="http://www.SRFsocialmedia.com"    class="socialmedia"    aria-label="   my
Socialmedia page" ></a>
```

What would help us in implementing a good useful solution to announce through various options such as visually hidden? Let us take few examples to analyze the implementations.

Best Example: Actionable (Linked) Background Image with Alternative Text via CSS Clip

In our sample website of SRF Web Accessibility Project, assume that the Socialmedia icon is a link that appears as a CSS background image. Because background pictures do not provide alt attributes, the link uses the "clipped approach" to hide text that is visible to the naked eye but accessible to screen readers. In such circumstances, it's worth noting that the text isn't obscured by utilizing visibility: Because these approaches also hide the text from screen reassembly, hidden or display: none is recommended. Refer the sample html snippet:

```
<a href="https://www.SRFsocialmedia.com" class="Socialmedia_icon"> <span class="visually hidden">My Socialmedia page</span>
</a>
```

The markup for the CSS:

```
.socialmedia_icon {
background-image: url("socialmedia.png"); background-color: #00274d;
height: 29px;
width: 29px;
display: inline-block;}

visually-hidden {
border: 0;
clip: rect(0000);
height: 1px;
margin: -1px;
overflow: hidden;
padding: 0;
position: absolute;
width: 1px;}
```

Bad Example (Not Recommended): Actionable (Linked) Background Image with No Alternative Text

There is an integrated Socialmedia link in the background image, but no alternate text for a screen reader to relay to a user. By reading some or all of the href content, most screen readers will attempt to convey context about the link to the user. As you smay expect, some href text isn't very descriptive of the location.

```
<a href="https://www.SRFsocialmedia.com/My page" class="socialmedia_icon"></a>
```

Bad Example (Not Recommended): Background Image Has Hidden Text Using Visibility Hidden

While there is text in the HTML to replace the background picture, screen readers disregard the text when it is hidden with visibility hidden.

```
<div class="tw" id="Icon">
<a href="http://www.SRFsocialmedia.com">
<span class="visually-hidden2">Our Socialmedia page</span>
</a>
</div>
.visually-hidden2 {
visibility:hidden;
}
.tw {
background-image:url("assets/images/reference/socialmedia.png");
width: 29px;
background-height: 29px;
background-position: left;
padding-left:35px;
background-repeat:no-repeat;
}
```

Bad Example (Not Recommended): Background Image Has Hidden Text Using Display:none

In the same way that visibility:hidden makes text unavailable to screen reader users, display:none makes text unavailable to screen reader users.

```
<div class="tw" id="Icon">
<a href="http://www.SRFsocialmedia.com">
<span class="visually-hidden3">Our Socialmedia page</span>
</a>
</div>
.visually-hidden3 (
display:none;}

.tw {
background-image:url("assets/images/reference/socialmedia_png");
width: 29px;
background-height: 29px;
background-position:left;
padding-left:35px;
background-repeat:no-repeat;
}
```

An Art Accessibility

Yamini continues to explain some examples on handling the art images while selling some gallery or products through SRF websites. She suggested that depending on how the developer plans to utilize the picture, it can be described in a variety of ways. Let us take an example of alt text details for a gallery image of painting get sold through SRF website.

The Alt Text

Even if a comprehensive description is provided, the image will require alt text when displayed on the website. It's also possible to note that a longer description is available elsewhere in the alt text. One option is presented below if the goal is to show the picture to consumers and discuss the artist's intended meaning. Remember that the alt text should be brief, and the long description should be easily accessible to users by placing it on the page, or in a separate web page accessible via a link below the image, or in a popup dialog accessible via a button below the image, or in some other method that is easy to find and access.

Option 1: Short alt text

alt="Indian painting is one of the oldest arts in the world from about the 3rd millennium BC to present period"

Option 2: Short alt text, with a reference to the long description

alt="Indian painting is one of the oldest arts in the world from about the 3rd millennium BC to present period and famous as well".

Option 3: More detailed alt text

alt="Indian painting is one of the oldest arts in the world from about the 3rd millennium BC to present period. The society the Indian painting reproduce particular religious, political and cultural developments."

Note: Any of the choices listed above can be used. The brief alt text would necessitate a longer, easy-to-find description. The longer alt text may be sufficient on its own, making the lengthy description unnecessary.

The long description

Only if the author's aim requires more explanation than a quick alt text allows is a long description of the painting required.

A long description can be presented to consumers in a variety of ways:

- Put the long description in a paragraph below the image on the web page.
- Add a link to a page that has the extended description. "Detailed description of image," for example, may be the link text.
- Make a button that opens a dialog box with the lengthy description. "Show comprehensive description," for example, might be written on the button.
- Add a button below the image that extends a long description. The description would be concealed at first, but once the user activated the button, it would become visible. "Expand to display extensive description," for example, might be written on the button.

Option 1: An Objective Long Description with as Little Interpretation as Possible

alt="Indian painting is one of the oldest arts in the world from about the 3rd millennium BC to present period. The society the Indian painting reproduce particular religious, political and cultural developments.

Indian art has its unique place in the history of arts. Indian art has been challenged for its stage from down to the top of winning the stage of philosophy under the visual type in the history of Indian art.

Option 2: An interpretive description

alt= "Indian painting is one of the oldest arts in the world from about the 3rd millennium BC to present period. The society the Indian painting reproduce particular religious, political and cultural developments. Indian art has its unique name in the history of arts. Indian art which has been challenged its stage from down to the top of winning the stage of philosophy under the visual type in the history of Indian art. Indian art has challenging in the years in thought providing in the Indian artist in the reason for the innovation of the creations in the way of visual abstracts ideas and the cultured thing in the land."

Medical, Health, or Ecology Images Accessibility

The image to be described in this section is shown below:

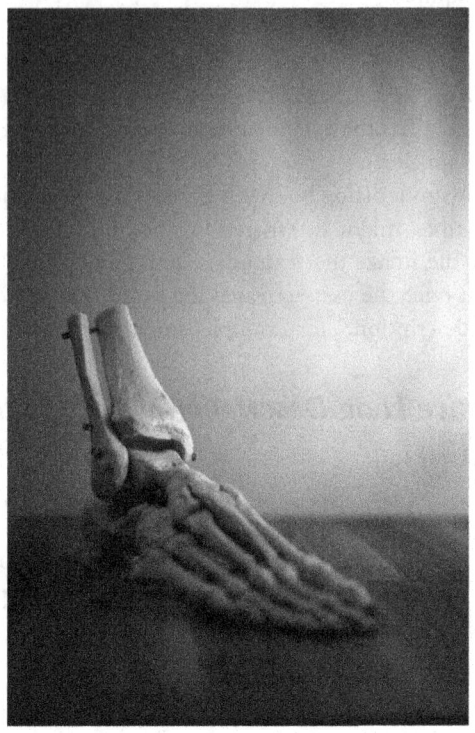

Picture: Closeup of Skeleton Foot Model[20].

After seeing this image, Sandhya initially was scared and decided to use it slowly since it is one of the requirements to be added into their photo sales section of the SRF online sales store. But she panicked to think on alt text. Yes, it's too scary for her to keep looking at it and imagining about right alt text and Yamini came to help her on time once again.

Option 1: Short alt text

A longer description would need to be added to this alt text.

alt="The fingers of our hands have are the most useful feature and the ones we use most"

Option 2. More Detailed Alt Text

Depending on the author's intention. It's possible that this longer alt text is all that's needed.

alt="The fingers of our hands have are the most useful feature and the ones we use most. The bones of the human hand are comprised into 3 main sections"

The Long Description

Example : A Detailed Long Description

Note: A literal description like this would be useful in circumstances when the user is requested to interpret the diagram, such as a learning assessment. In other cases, a less extensive description may be appropriate.

The fingers of our hands have the most useful feature and the ones we use most. The first finger of the hand is the Index finger it is usually the most agile finger as it has the most use. The second finger of the hand is the middle finger, by itself the middle finger has only one major use attributed to it, a very vulgar hand signal. Moving down to the ring finger, as its name suggests it is used for wearing a wedding ring in western culture.

Web-based Map Directions and Accessibility

After discussing about art gallery images, Mark raised a question on how to handle map images or directions to provide accessibility since some of the services and branches of SRF are listed with map location of the properties across the US and the UK. Now Yamini takes help from CBK and few other specialists to explain the complexities involved in testing maps. Maps are, by their very nature, a visual concept. They are two-dimensional spatial representations of physical spaces, frequently with embedded symbols and unique meanings associated with different line kinds (e.g., representing streets, buildings, etc.). Maps have a complete visual lexicon that is challenging to express to visually impaired people. The audience is also expected to be able to perceive the spatial relationships between objects.

There's also the issue that maps can be utilized for a variety of purposes. A map can be used to acquire a feel of a city's layout, to learn the name of a building, to determine how close locations are to one another, to locate the nearest bus stop, to locate a coffee shop, or to obtain instructions from one spot to another. It's impossible to foresee how someone will utilize a map.

Creating meaningful, well-written alternative text for all of the possible uses of a map is essentially impossible. Fortunately, the alternative text for some map uses can be automated by data and algorithms, such as the creation of driving directions.

You might ask: Why would a blind person require driving directions? They are unable to drive since they are blind. While they cannot drive alone, they can act as navigators for their drivers or describe directions to others so that they can drive themselves. We shouldn't draw erroneous assumptions about persons who are blind simply because the data is visually oriented. Let us take an example map image from a phone:

Picture: Travel Map from a Phone Map[21].

Visual Directions

Let us look at another example in this section as a map direction:

In theory, the visual aspects of the directions (where things are spatially and visually in relation to one another) can be described, but this would almost certainly necessitate intelligent writing by a human who was aware of how the directions would be used and which types of visual information would be required for blind users. Since CBK himself having 70% vision loss, he mentioned that maps are really complex to handle along with Talkback of his android phones. Although we may not be able to provide alternate text for all of a map's probable uses, we must remember that good color contrast and customizable color selections will aid the low vision community and color-blind users.

Text Direction Accessibility

When a user types these directions into Bing, the visual depiction of the pathway appears on the map itself. The driving directions are written on the left side of the page in a sidebar. These instructions are also available in a printable format. Bing's directions are only available in text format.

Text instructions, such as those in the example above, are an excellent technique to make map directions available to screen reader users assuming that the map application interface is

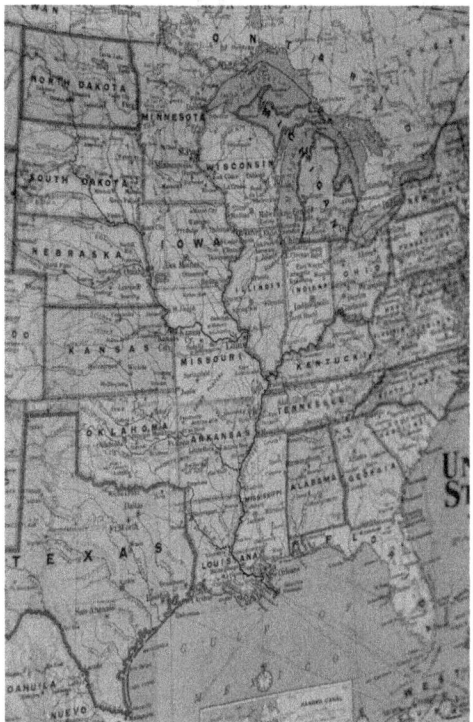

Picture: Image of a Map[22].

completely accessibility. The basic idea of transforming a visual experience (maps) into a different format (a list) will be applied to other types of visual information as well. So CBK suggested Naren to have a thorough testing on maps with different combinations of screen reader and zooming tools to make sure that the best practices are getting implemented.

SVG Accessibility

Now let us look at another important question from Claire to Yamini in this section. Claire got a request from customer to update SVG image of product in their grocery sales site and she want Yamini to guide her team. Yamini continues with her inputs on SVG graphics:

SVG includes a lot of factors that make graphics more accessible on the web. They are especially useful for those who are blind or have poor eyesight and use assistive technology, as well as people who have color blindness. The accessibility properties of SVG have the added benefit of increasing the usability of data for those without disabilities, such as those who access the web via mobile devices or other non-traditional devices, such as tablets.

This section concentrates on SVG's accessibility features. It is not meant to go over all of the different ways to create and use SVG. A compendium of SVG information, a highly thorough reference, may provide details on everything from fundamental implementation to gradients, animations, and all kinds of other goodies.

What are Scalable Vector Graphics?

SVG is vector-based graphics format that is defined in XML and it is also a two-dimensional graphics. They can be written and changed with a text editor, but graphic editing software like Adobe Illustrator or Inkscape is more likely. SVU is a language in and of itself, akin to HTML, and was initially introduced by the World Wide Web Consortium (W3C) in 1999. Unfortunately, due to a lack of web browsing, SVU has not been widely used for graphic design up to this moment. Most recent browsers now support it, albeit there may be some differences in how they are understood by different types of screen readers. In addition, it should be mentioned that Internet Explorer does not allow animation.

Vector structures, such as paths with straight lines or curves, are among the three types of graphical elements that can be created with SVG. It is also possible to create graphics and text. SVG can also be interactive and dynamic, with animations activated declaratively by embedding them inline or via scripting.

SVG objects are resolution independent, so they'll appear just as good on a smaller smartphone as they will on a desktop computer with a 24-inch monitor. This is especially important for people with impaired vision and those who use assistive technology with low resolution. Furthermore, because the picture is constructed using mathematical principles, it will scale flawlessly irrespective of whether it is extended or compressed, making SVG the best choice for responsive design.

Raster versus Vector Graphic

When Magnified, Vector Images Retain their Sharpness

A raster image, also known as a bitmap, is made up of a collection of dots or pixels, each having its own color value. On the other hand, vector images are built out of basic geometric objects like lines, points, and curves, and their relationship is based on mathematical formulae. As a result, regardless of the zoom factor or quality, vector graphics will scale properly. The image will be clean and unaltered.

When you zoom closer on raster images, they get "pixelated," which means they become hazy or deformed. Depending on the action taken on the image, the pixels are stretched or reduced. Raster images, on the other hand, have a place because they are the best format for complex pictures like photographs.

Vector images, on the other hand, are best used for simple drawings like line art, logos, charts and graphs, or text.

Now coming back to our favorite web accessibility project, Yamini's detailed sessions on images accessibility made Naren to write good amount of manual tests against image verifications. He also went on to discuss with BA Juliet to incorporate acceptance criteria of every user story related to image enhancement to update right accessibility checks as definition of done (DOD).

In this section, we learnt about different usage of accessibility guidelines and best practices on image and pictures when displayed on websites through Yamini, Naren, CBK, Claire, Mark, and few other best engineers part of Web Accessibility Project. Thank you for being patient enough to read through different examples and scenarios to understand the tips and tricks. Let us learn about some of the accessibility test automation techniques in next part of the book.

We are circling back to the closure of Web Accessibility Project's Manual Testing Scopes in this chapter but Naren is not going to end his accessibility tests anytime soon since accessibility tests are ongoing and repetitive efforts to check against latest Government Policies and International Guidelines. He also realized that he tested many SRF websites in the past against WCAG version 2.0 and 2.1 in different occasions but he wanted to repeat testing when WCAG 3.0 released in coming years. At this stage, let us bid adieu to our favorite SRF project engineers.

Notes

1. "I'm in a popular website(name removed)! And the accessibility issue is…" YouTube video, [duration in 00:01:13],Transcript source https://habengirma.com/transcripts/national_geographic_transcript.txt Posted by "Haben Girma" (August 22, 2021), video source: https://www.youtube.com/watch?app=desktop&v=hx92cScWG6s
2. Title: Using aria-labelledby to provide a text alternative for non-text content. (January 9, 2014). Retrieved from https://www.w3.org/WAI/GL/wiki/Using_aria-labelledby_to_provide_a_text_alternative_for_non-text_content
3. Title: WAI-ARIA Roles. (Accessed 12 December 2021). Retrieved from https://developer.mozilla.org/en-US/docs/Web/Accessibility/ARIA/Roles
4. Title: An alt Decision Tree. (Updated July 27, 2019) (first published September 2014). (Accessed 12 December 2021). Retrieved from https://www.w3.org/WAI/tutorials/images/decision-tree/
5. Andreas Palmer. (June 12, 2017) Free to use under the Unsplash License. (Accessed 12 December 2021). Available at: https://unsplash.com/photos/UJSjxFNLFWY
6. Dan Gold. (March 18, 2017) Free to use under the Unsplash License. (Accessed 12 December 2021). Available at: https://unsplash.com/s/photos/car?utm_source=unsplash&utm_medium=referral&utm_content=creditCopyText
7. Johann Siemens. (June 11, 2014) Free to use under the Unsplash License. (Accessed 12 December 2021). Available at: https://unsplash.com/photos/EPy0gBJzzZU
8. Narayanan Palani (December 11, 2021) Image of NP Logo (Accessed 12 December 2021).
9. Matt Artz. (November 12, 2018) Free to use under the Unsplash License. (Accessed 12 December 2021). Available at: https://unsplash.com/photos/YPd84QSltZ8
10. Joel Herzog. (June 29, 2016) Free to use under the Unsplash License. (Accessed 12 December 2021). Available at: https://unsplash.com/photos/2_5IXdiwmyM
11. Joshua Hoehne. (February 17, 2021) Free to use under the Unsplash License. (Accessed 12 December 2021). Available at: https://unsplash.com/photos/Nsaqv7v2V7Q
12. Markus Winkler. (June 9, 2020) Free to use under the Unsplash License. (Accessed 12 December 2021). Available at: https://unsplash.com/photos/IrRbSND5EUc
13. Title: Providing a link to the long description via longdesc. (Updated July 27, 2019) (first published September 2014). (Accessed 12 December 2021). Retrieved from https://www.w3.org/WAI/tutorials/images/complex/#providing-a-link-to-the-long-description-via-longdesc
14. Tech Daily(@TechDailyCA). (February 22, 2021) Free to use under the Unsplash License. (Accessed 12 December 2021). Available at: https://unsplash.com/photos/ztYmIQecyH4
15. Narayanan Palani (December 11, 2021) Image of NP Logo (Accessed 12 December 2021).
16. Thiébaud Faix. (December 1, 2018) Free to use under the Unsplash License. (Accessed 12 December 2021). Available at: https://unsplash.com/photos/eBkEJ9cH5b4
17. Thiébaud Faix. (December 1, 2018) Free to use under the Unsplash License. (Accessed 12 December 2021). Available at: https://unsplash.com/photos/eBkEJ9cH5b4
18. Title: Using CSS to replace text with images of text and providing user interface controls to switch. (Accessed 12 December 2021). Retrieved from https://www.w3.org/WAI/WCAG21/Techniques/css/C30.html
19. Alice. (March 19, 2021) Free to use under the Unsplash License. (Accessed 12 December 2021). Available at: https://unsplash.com/photos/ALoh02V8eaE

20. Otto Norin. (March 15, 2021) Free to use under the Unsplash License. (Accessed 12 December 2021). Available at: https://unsplash.com/photos/FAdw0aRMXp4
21. Tamas Tuzes-Katai. (November 2, 2020) Free to use under the Unsplash License. (Accessed 12 December 2021). Available at: https://unsplash.com/photos/rEn-AdBr3Ig
22. Hans Isaacson. (May 31, 2021) Free to use under the Unsplash License. (Accessed 12 December 2021). Available at: https://unsplash.com/photos/hAJhORQHk94code>

AUTOMATED WEB ACCESSIBILITY DEVELOPMENT AND TESTING

B

Chapter 18

Cypress JavaScript Test Automation Framework Setup

CypressIO is one of the popular JavaScript based open source test automation tool (their dashboard service is licensed which is optional for the users) and it helps in performing some fastest accessibility audits using plugins, such as cypress-axe, cypress-lighthouse, and cypress-audit. There are new innovative plugins getting added throughout the years hence please touch base with CypressIO plugins directory[2] to check latest plugins available for testing different functionalities and testing types.

While installing first time, it may display a dialog box in which "Allow Access" needs to be clicked to enable it to get executed on the target website:

Take Few Minutes to Setup the Cypress Framework

The complete code is ready for this article and all you need is to use the repository to install by cloning from github at "Cypress Test Techniques." and run tests.

Installation Steps

Make sure to have nodejs (version 14+) installed in the laptop. It just takes 5 minutes to setup Cypress framework

1. npm install
2. npm link
3. npm link cypress-cucumber-preprocessor
4. npm install through

Please refer to this fully developed repository made available as open source code to help you learning Cypress test automation. README file from the repository can be referred for further installation instructions: "Cypress Test Techniques."[3]

DOI: 10.1201/9781003299431-20

Picture: Windows Defender Firewall Notification to Unblock CypressIO to Run Tests in Windows Laptops.

An alternative code repository provided to enhance API tests into Cypress framework to extend API verifications earlier in life cycle: "Cypress API Test Techniques."[4]

Detailed code examples and end to end test types are provided in the book earlier on "Automated Software Testing with Cypress."[5]

Let us look at some code examples in the next chapter on how cypress-axe based automated accessibility scans help in preventing accessibility violations.

Notes

1. Title: CypressIO JavaScript End to End Testing Framework. Retrieved from https://www.cypress.io/
2. Title: CypressIO Plugins Directory. Retrieved from https://docs.cypress.io/plugins/directory
3. Title: Cypress Test Techniques. (Accessed 12 December 2021). Retrieved from https://github.com/narayananpalani/cypress-test-techniques
4. Title: Cypress API Test Techniques. (Accessed 12 December 2021). Retrieved from https://github.com/narayananpalani/cypress-api-test-techniques
5. Title: Automated Software Testing with Cypress. Retrieved from https://www.taylorfrancis.com/books/mono/10.1201/9781003145110/automated-software-testing-cypress-narayan-palani

Chapter 19

Cypress Accessibility Testing using Cypress-Audit

During the past 3 years, accessibility has been integrated to web development requirements for majority of the organizations due to the legislation efforts and guidelines narrated by Web Content Accessibility Guidelines (WCAG), Section 508 (USA), The Americans with Disabilities Act (ADA), European Accessibility Act (EAA), and regulations from each country that recommends the organizations to adhere to certain level of accessibility standards. On the flip side, not may front-end engineers and QAs are really aware of what it really means.

There are hefty penalties for organizations if they are failing to meet the accessibility guidelines and we can see the news all around the world on the customer complaints due to the poor behavior from few websites when accessed through assistive technologies.

Is Accessibility Meant only for Developers to Focus?

A majority of the QAs are in assumption that as long as developers taking care of the attributes and update the websites, it will work for better accessibility and getting them tested through functional tests are good enough to move on for live deployment. It is a common misunderstanding that is leading to poor customer experience.

My recent survey in LinkedIn suggests that accessibility is everybody's responsibility within the feature team:

Accessibility is a "test and learn" subject and unless it is tested with screen reader, there is no way one can tell what will the customer experience when they access it.

Where to Start?

An highly advanced agile team starts thinking about accessibility right from PI Planning (Program Increment Planning) to segregate and align related epics and user stories to produce high-quality

DOI: 10.1201/9781003299431-21

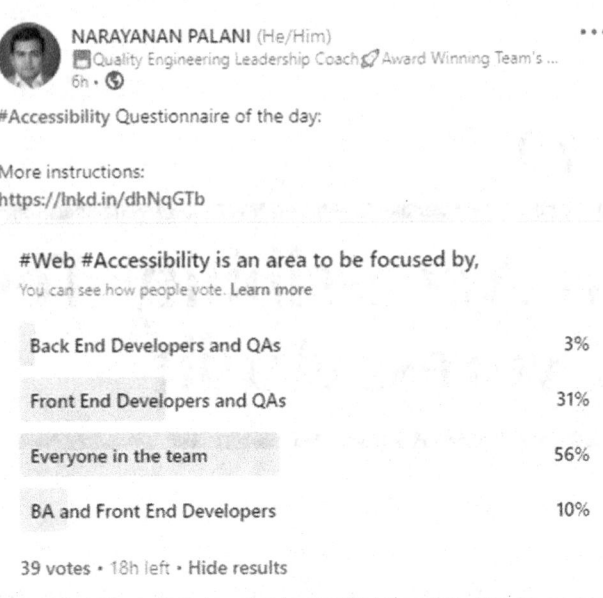

Picture: LinkedIn Survey of Narayanan Palani on Accessibility Focus[1].

(inclusive) design and accessibility-focused web development. Hence, accessibility testing starts from a design review onward.

Where to Start the Actual Accessibility Testing?

When a web page is built in front-end engineers' workspace (either laptop or their cloud space), that's when the accessibility audit (first level test) needs to be conducted to start finding first hand defects.

What Tools to Use for Accessibility Audit?

As a industry leading solution, Axe is the best tool from Deque to test the web pages against WCAG standards and they have got it integrated with CypressIO, a famous JavaScript Automation Tool for Unit Integration Test and System Integrated Test needs.

Based on my LinkedIn poll, cypress-audit and cypress-axe are most used plugins to test the accessibility audit checks early on:

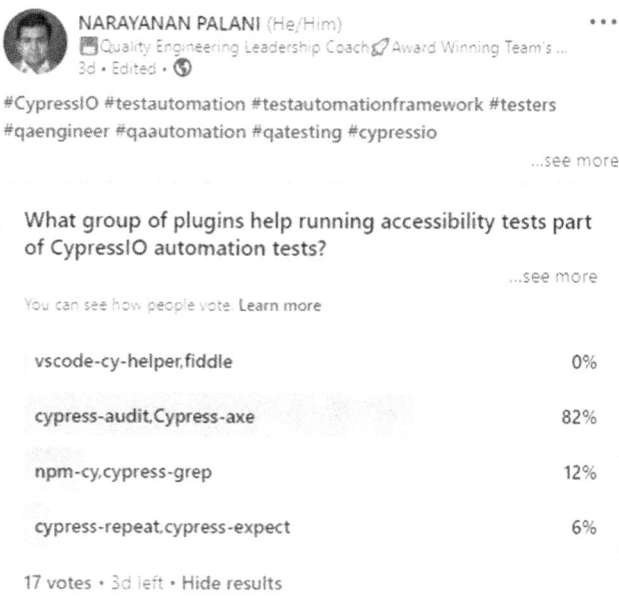

Picture: Linkedin Survey on Cypress Plugins[2].

What are Some of the Critical Defects Impacting User Eye Sight and Health in General?

When a user has some sort of vision loss or color blindness, seeing a color which has poor color contrast will impact these users due to the frequent eye strain and my recent survey in LinkedIn suggests that color should not be the primary differentiator for web page links (when hover over) since color blind users would not differentiate it when the focus is on those links:

How to perform a basic cypress-axe test in CypressIO?

CypressIO-based JavaScript tests are super fast and compatible to run in CI/CD in a easiest possible way.

The first step is to build the framework and add an import in Index.js:

```
import 'cypress-axe'
```

While launching the url, I used inject code to enable cypress-axe during the test:

```
launchPage () {
  cy.visit('/')
    .injectAxe()
},
```

Written a small feature File to check the accessibility violation in Gherkin format:

Picture: Linkedin Survey on Color Blindness[3].

```
Feature: Recruitment page a11y checks

Scenario: Verify a11y violations on recruitment tab
 Given I open homepage
 When I SignIn as user
 And I click on Recruitment tab of home page
 Then I perform accessibility audit using axe
```

Step Definition to support the audit violation checks:

```
Given('I perform accessibility audit using axe', () => {
 loginOrangehrmPage.a11yAuditAxe()
})
```

Function written to verify the accessibility violations through checkA11y function:

```
a11yAuditAxe () {
  cy.checkA11y(null, null, terminalLog)
},
```

Ideally in a simple code of single page verification (with no requirement to go to any additional pages), this code (mentioned above) works as expected to produce the accessibility violations. But it won't be the same if you run the same function to check a page after navigating from first few pages dynamically and the same code fails with an error below.

Error:

Cannot read property 'run' of undefined

The primary reason is that the injectAxe needs to be called for a page to inject axe first and perform accessibility checks through checkA11y() after that. Hence I slightly modified the function with a fix:

```
a11yAuditAxe () {
  cy.injectAxe()
  cy.checkA11y(null, null, terminalLog)
},
```

Use this command to run tests:

npx cypress run--spec cypress\integration\features\recruitmentOrangehrmA11yAudit.feature--browser chrome

Test Results:

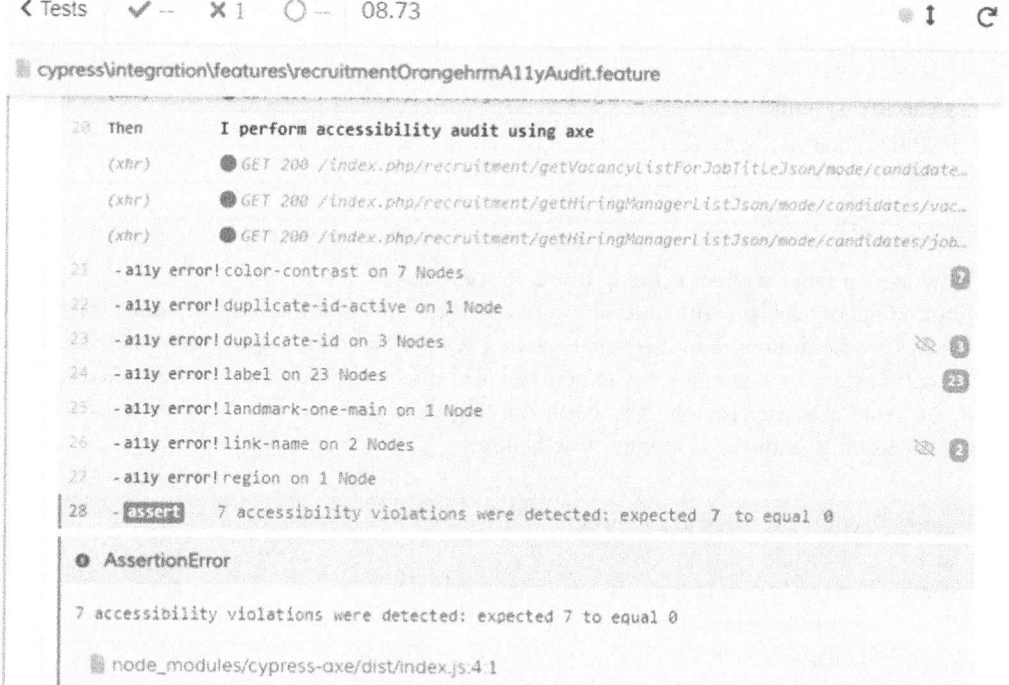

Picture: Cypress Test with Assertion Error.

Identifying most critical bugs of the code:

Most of the times, just using checkA11y command is not of much use since the project priorities may be different at different occasions. While just deploying before final live deployments, if you want to check just critical bugs in accessibility, it can be customized with the code below.

Feature File:

Feature: Recruitment page a11y checks

Scenario: Verify a11y critical violations on recruitment tab
 Given I open OrangeHRM homepage
 When I SignIn as user
 And I click on Recruitment tab of home page
 Then I perform accessibility audit using axe to check critical violations

Step Definition:

```
Given('I perform accessibility audit using axe to check critical violations', () => {
  loginOrangehrmPage.a11yAuditAxeCritical()
})
```

Function:

```
a11yAuditAxeCritical () {
  cy.injectAxe()
  cy.checkA11y(null,{
    includedImpacts: ['critical']
  }, terminalLog)
},
```

How to skip failures when running multiple scenarios?

Another major problem with accessibility audits is that the first test fails the whole feature file and when QAs hold more than 20+ scenarios in a feature file, there is possibility that the entire test execution stops by just one scenario getting failed due to the violations found in accessibility audit. To avoid this interruption, it is worth running the tests even after receiving the violations part of accessibility audit by skipping those failures:

Feature: Recruitment page a11y checks

Scenario: Verify a11y violations on recruitment tab
 Given I open OrangeHRM homepage
 When I SignIn as user
 And I click on Recruitment tab of home page

Then I perform accessibility audit using axe by skipping failures

Step Definition:

```
Given('I perform accessibility audit using axe by skipping failures', () => {
  loginOrangehrmPage.a11yAuditAxeSkipFail()
})
```

Function:

```
a11yAuditAxeSkipFail () {
  cy.injectAxe()
  cy.checkA11y(null, null, terminalLog,{skipFailures: true})
},
```

Execution:
Even though violations are present, test skips failures and move on to the next scenario:

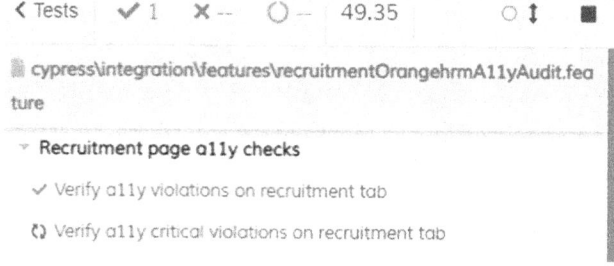

Picture: Cypress Test Displays a First Test as Pass and Running Next Test.

Customize with relevant guidelines:
It is also possible to customize the code to check just few selective components or UI properties, such as tags using following configuration:

```
{
  runOnly: {
    type: 'tag',
    values: ['wcag2a']
  }
}
```

Let us see how to implement such features in the cucumber-based cypress tests:
Feature file:

Feature: Recruitment page a11y checks

Scenario: Verify a11y violations on recruitment tab to check tags as per wcag
 Given I open OrangeHRM homepage
 When I SignIn as user
 And I click on Recruitment tab of home page
 Then I perform accessibility audit using axe to check tags as per wcag

Step Definitions:

Given('I perform accessibility audit using axe to check tags as per wcag', ()
=> {
   loginOrangehrmPage.a11yAuditAxeCheckTags()
})

Function:

```
a11yAuditAxeCheckTags () {
  cy.injectAxe()
  cy.checkA11y(null,{
  runOnly: {
    type: 'tag',
    values: ['wcag2a']
  }
  }, terminalLog)
},
```

This time the test produces violations related to WCAG2A:

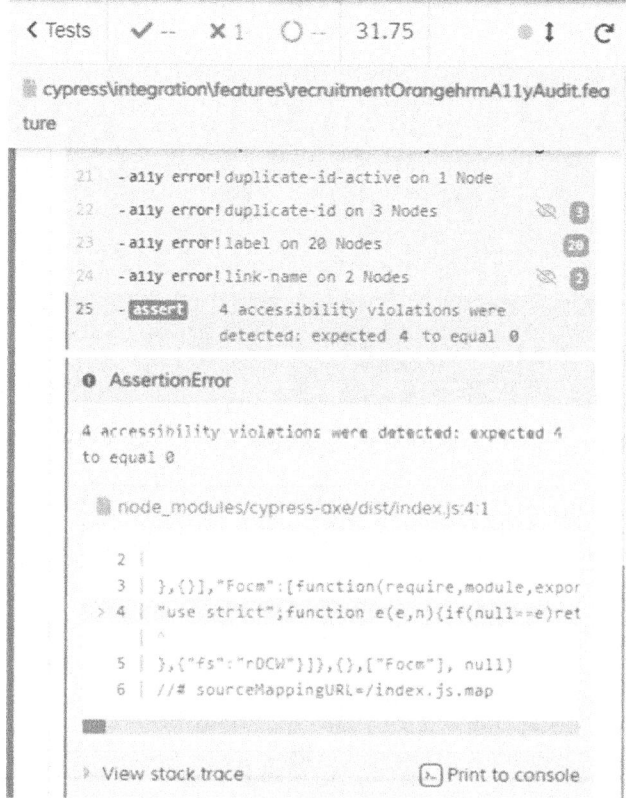

Picture: Cypress Displays Four Accessibility Violations.

But it is recommended to add more appropriate values to include Section 508 and wcag2aa:

```
a11yAuditAxeCheckTags () {
  cy.injectAxe()
  cy.checkA11y(null,{
   runOnly: {
     type: 'tag',
     values: ['wcag2aa', 'wcag2a', 'section508']
   }
 }, terminalLog)
},
```

Results:

Picture: Cypress Displays Five Accessibility Violations.

If you carefully look at the function, I used terminalLog enabled most of the time:

```
// Define at the top of the spec file or just import it
function terminalLog(violations) {
 cy.task(
   'log',
   '${violations.length} accessibility violation${
     violations.length === 1 ? '' : 's'
   } ${violations.length === 1 ? 'was' : 'were'} detected`
 )
// pluck specific keys to keep the table readable
const violationData = violations.map(
   ({ id, impact, description, nodes }) => ({
   id,
   impact,
   description,
   nodes: nodes.length
   })
 )
```

```
cy.task('table', violationData)
}

// Then in your test...
it('Logs violations to the terminal', () => {
  cy.checkA11y(null, null, terminalLog)
})
```

Thanks to the plugin creator of Cypress-axe here: https://github.com/component-driven/cypress-axe

These terminal logs configuration help in getting the test results into the terminal of IDE from where you are running the tests:

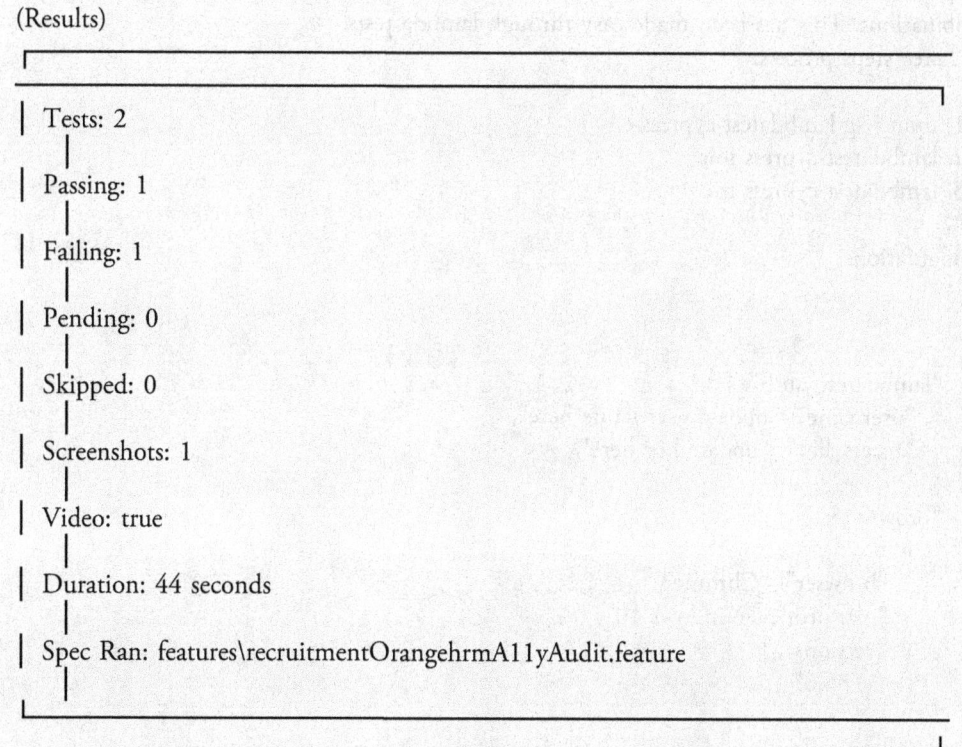

(Results)

```
┌────────────────────────────────────────────────────────────────────┐
│ Tests: 2                                                             │
│                                                                      │
│ Passing: 1                                                           │
│                                                                      │
│ Failing: 1                                                           │
│                                                                      │
│ Pending: 0                                                           │
│                                                                      │
│ Skipped: 0                                                           │
│                                                                      │
│ Screenshots: 1                                                       │
│                                                                      │
│ Video: true                                                          │
│                                                                      │
│ Duration: 44 seconds                                                 │
│                                                                      │
│ Spec Ran: features\recruitmentOrangehrmA11yAudit.feature            │
│                                                                      │
└────────────────────────────────────────────────────────────────────┘
```

(Screenshots)

- F:\cypressSetup\cypress-test-techniques\cypress\screenshots\features\recruitment (1366x613)
  OrangehrmA11yAudit.feature\Recruitment page a11y checks -- Verify a11y critical

  violations on recruitment tab (failed).png

Key Lessons: Accessibility is a Core Future of Test Automation

Due to the recent changes in the law and regulations of major governments across the US, the UK, Canada, Australia, and other countries, accessibility testing takes a priority when comparing to rest of the testing types. Equality Act 2010 and disability are taken seriously in international law through each countries own regulation, hence testing applications designed for end user needs accessibility as a core check. When bringing accessibility to testing world, automation of those accessibility are not necessarily important. Reason being, most of the accessibility needs have to be tested using screen readers and assistive technologies.

Readers are requested to watch relevant YouTube video to test accessibility guidelines through keyboard tests[4].

Run Cross Browser Tests in Cloud

Running tests in local is just a start with cypress framework but it is not good enough to verify complete stability of the code until it has been verified in different browser and operating system combinations. This has been made easy through lambda tests.

Three steps process:

1. npm i -g lambdatest-cypress-cli
2. lambdatest-cypress init
3. lambdatest-cypress run

Configuration:

```
{
   "lambdatest_auth": {
      "username": "update user name here",
      "access_key": "update key here"
   },
   "browsers": [
      {
         "browser": "Chrome",
         "platform": "Windows 10",
         "versions": [
            "86.0"
         ]
      },
      {
         "browser": "Firefox",
         "platform": "Windows 10",
         "versions": [
            "82.0",
            "81.0"
         ]
      }
```

```
    ],
    "run_settings": {
      "cypress_config_file": "cypress.json",
      "build_name": "hrmTestBetaV1.0.1",
      "parallels": 1,
      "specs": "./cypress/integration/features/homeOrangehrmTest.feature",
      "ignore_files": "",
      "feature_file_suppport": true,
      "network": false,
      "video": true
    },
    "tunnel_settings": {
      "tunnel": false,
      "tunnelName": null
    }
}
```

Key Lessons: Automate Accessibility Scans Regularly

Recently, I implemented AxeDevTools[5] (licensed tool which is the latest version of axe part of selenium tests) in my test code and it is running relentlessly to capture the application code violations against accessibility guidelines and getting a detailed test report to share it to developers to cross check the violations. But accessibility code scan itself is not an 100% automation of accessibility tests. After code scan, I spend good amount of time with screen readers to read the web pages with different keyboard shortcuts and test the behavior against WCAG 2.1 guidelines and analyze the confusing items and log defects to influence developers to fix the gaps and give better experience for end customers. Hence, re-writing same defects fixes, object property updates (like aria-label, title, id, aria-labelledby, etc.) through automated tests is helping me to find failures when those objects are corrupted during the code merges later in the stages. Hence writing accessibility code scan tests, manual accessibility tests, and automated accessibility regression tests are really useful for my code health checks toward accessibility guidelines coverage.

Key Lessons: False Positives from Accessibility Audits

More exceptions are expected to come in any of the accessibility audit tests. Even if you are using different tools, such as pa11y, you may still experience some amount of false positives but there is no choice at the moment in the industry except to filter them by exclude: config in tests. Nevertheless, it is worth getting enough reporting with detailed classification for each UI components to get a full view of the accessibility adherence. Both cypress-axe for CypressIO and axeDevTools for selenium provide a good level of reporting while testing through automation test code.

Key Lessons: It's is Not About Quantity of Tests, it is About Quality of those Tests in Accessibility Testing

Test reporting and test automation coverage statistics are most common measurements in agile teams and quantifying number of tests being written is the first formula of measurement as well as first mistake team does on their automation efforts. Yes, when number of test automation scripts are counted periodically, it won't give insights around the overall scenario coverage, coverage of edge cases and possibility of improving the tests toward untouched code. Hence the measurement of test automation scripts need to follow a pragmatic approach of test code stability. It means, how many times the test has shown a **consistent pass rate** during accessibility audits and accessibility regression tests when application code is not changed. If this stability has been reached, the next step is to explore possibilities of what more tests can be added. Most of the teams does a common mistake by running the cypress-axe or axeDevTools-based tests that always fail and provide violations in most test runs but QAs never update the scripts to exclude the false positives through their configurations, hence it leads to be given less attention to accessibility violation tests in the long run since most of the time it shows test failure when poorly maintained.

"Consistency is everything. Nothing happens when a script is written. But it has to be consistently maintained, executed and updated time to time."

Key Lessons: Automate the Defect Retests

When (application) defects are identified from automated test failures, the first impression is to retest them when they are fixed and move towards a regression testing phase. But forgetting to automate the (accessibility) defect retest itself is a costly mistake. Reason being, when a defect has been retested, highly likely that the same branch of the (accessibility) defect fix code may be missed in later code merges or slipped to merge in the right code version to reach the end users. Unless this has been written as an automated test with right tags to get tested from there on, it will be an easy escape for this defect(later in the releases) to live with the code forever. Of course not all the steps can be automated as selenium or CypressIO tests but some UI attributes can be converted as automated regression tests.

"Sometimes in life, you're not always given a **second chance** but if you do, take advantage of it-Defect Retest is a second chance that gives you an opportunity to break the application once again."

No matter how many automated tests are written, it is impossible or inappropriate to skip screen readers-based manual tests. Since manual screen reader tests are the primary space to discover poor customer experience to check against accessibility guidelines.

"Even though calculator simplified our life, mathematicians still go for handwritten notes—that's always a power of muscle memory—similar to that no matter how many automated tests run in your pipeline like calculator, few manual a11y tests (similar to hand-written muscle memory experience) will produce interesting unexpected accessibility defects in first few minutes."

Testing website against accessibility is essential but verifying overall performance metrics across the loading time and accessibility score is critical to measure the overall betterment of the website to monitor its experience for a normal user when loading the site. If the website loads with extreme delay and left with poor accessibility score, it will lead to poor customer traction, hence let us learn about performance and accessibility metrics assessment in the next chapter.

Notes

1. Title: Accessibility Focus-Linkedin Survey. Retrieved from https://www.linkedin.com/posts/narayananpalani_accessibility-activity-6821384914517168128-HoK8
2. Title: Cypress Accessibility Plugins-Linkedin Survey. Retrieved from https://www.linkedin.com/posts/narayananpalani_cypressio-testautomation-testautomationframework-activity-6819962478559019008-eW1q
3. Title: Color Blindness-Linkedin Survey. Retrieved from https://www.linkedin.com/posts/narayananpalani_accessibility-activity-6820870667722883072-sxmD
4. "Accessibility Testing-Operable Keyboard Tab Sequence" YouTube video, [duration in 00:04:19] Posted by "Narayanan Palani" (4 Jul 2018), video source: https://www.youtube.com/watch?v=JOYRfohlNDc
5. Title: axe DevTools®. Retrieved from https://www.deque.com/axe/devtools/

Chapter 20

Cypress Lighthouse Performance Metrics and Accessibility Score

During this COVID-19 pandemic, websites and mobile apps are the primary source of access for daily household of many of us from medical appointments to food delivery. When websites are load extremely slow, it makes the customer to think about the alternatives.

When the local lockdowns were relaxed in the UK, I was keen to get a better deal on an international flight and tried booking tickets on the website and it was extremely slow in loading the prices and I lost best cheap deals on the return flights and eventually tickets were all sold out when I refreshed the page to fill forms, To my surprise, that popular flight website took 3 minutes to load its first interactive dropdowns to select the destination and the full page loaded only after 4 minutes; hence, the final price of the ticket changed when I reached the last page by entering full details. Thus, I lost an opportunity to travel and the tickets were sold out for the dates I was booking tickets for.

What are the Performance Metrics Standards for Websites?

The common standard of a front-end engineer on any NodeJS web application is 2 seconds load time of its first interactive content, such as text box or buttons and it has to be fixed if the first content load takes more than 2 seconds. Story is not over yet. Even when the page loads it, the complete page should get loaded in not more than 3 seconds.

Most of the front-end engineers and testers know that lighthouse plugin from Google Chrome is one of the powerful tools to get the performance score similar to performance tab of Chrome Dev Tools;

DOI: 10.1201/9781003299431-22

Metrics Type	Best Score/ Minimum Standards	Location of the tool
Performance Metrics Score	95%	Lighthouse plugin (from Google Chrome- More Tools > Developer Tools)
First Contentful Paint	Maximum 1–2 seconds	
Time to Interactive	Maximum 2–3 seconds	

Key Recommendations

- It is advisable to "disable cache" from network tab (inside Developer Tools of Google Chrome) and retry to get the metrics from lighthouse for more appropriate results.
- Lighthouse v6 is available from Google Chrome v84 onwards. It is also available as a plugin for test automation tools such as CypressIO.

In addition to lighthouse tab of Google Chrome, performance tab of developer tools is another best place to get insights into performance delays around scripting, rendering, painting, system, idle, etc.

Scripting is a key metric calculated to figure out on how fast the web pages are getting loaded; similarly rendering and painting CSS load time depends on the React Apps.

When websites like travel booking sites have loads of data dependency from their servers, it can take up to 2 seconds to script the page (analyzed through "scripting" of performance tab), it will be a poor experience when it crosses 4 seconds or more due to the extensive delay. Even if the site holds a huge list of data like a foreign exchange table and currency values when sending money to different currencies, it is worth to load within 2 seconds as scripting. But the site has to be interactive within 3 seconds for a better customer experience (irrelevant of heavy data dependencies and API calls).

Use CypressIO for a Fast and Seamless Test Execution Experience

During my tests of web applications in the year 2018, First Contentful Paint for majority of the travel websites was ranging from 3 to 6 seconds to load the websites and I chose to write scripts on CypressIO with an assumption that CypressIO helps in running the tests fast, hence I can avoid consuming more time and flakiness in tests to rerun tests multiple times. Recently, it has come up with a retry feature in which I can set a retry value as 2 in cypress.json to get the same test running twice when failing due to issues such as delayed load time.

Getting performance metrics for each page on its load time is extremely time-consuming since most of the web development projects deal with 40 to 200 web pages depends on the user journeys. This article helps you learn how to automate those webpages using CypressIO and lighthouse in Jenkins, hence verifying those performance metrics made extremely simple through a plugin called cypress-audit.

Learn to Use Cypress-Audit Early in the Life Cycle

Refer the GitHub project of this plugin here (link)

Once Cypress framework has been setup, perform installation using the command below:

npm install --save-dev cypress-audit

Alternatively, for yarn users the command as per GitHub open source repository is,

yarn add -D cypress-audit

Once installation is done through git bash or the terminal of the IDE, try adding the constant at index.js file inside plugins folder:

const {lighthouse, pa11y, prepareAudit} = require("cypress-audit");

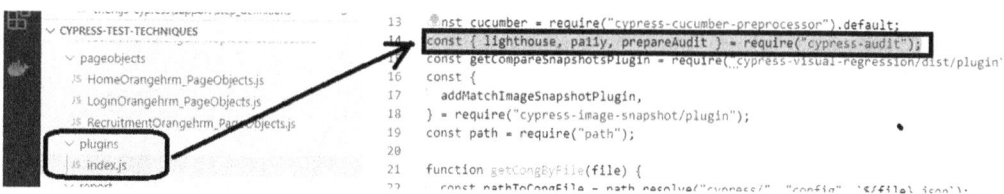

Picture: Image Representing the Constant Added to index.js at Plugins Folder of Cypress Framework.

Once index.js is updated, the next step is to start writing first feature file to verify the web audit results that include the performance metrics that we are interested in.

Feature: Login Page Verification on OrangeHRM website

Scenario: check web page health through lighthouse audit and pa11y audit on valid login page display with login fields
Given I open OrangeHRM homepage
Then I should see title "OrangeHRM"
Then I should see "LOGIN Panel" text displayed

And I should see "Alternative Login" text displayed
And I should see web audit results

After writing feature file, it takes 30 seconds to write a step definition in a shared js file for common usage across the framework as below:

```
Then('I should see web audit results', function () {
  cy.lighthouse();
})
```

Now our first test is ready partially. That's right. It is not yet 100% accurate since we are yet to measure the performance of the website against the standards that we want to verify against. Hence setting the threshold for the tests will make the results pass or fail as per the organization standards.

This can be done in two ways:

Option 1: Add thresholds within the step definition as below:

```
Then('I should see web audit results', function () {
  cy.lighthouse({
    performance: 95,
    accessibility: 100,
    "best-practices": 95,
    seo: 85,
    pwa: 100,
  }
  );
})
```

It is time for to run the tests
Let me run my tests with very simple command as,

```
npx cypress open
```

```
Windows PowerShell
Copyright (C) Microsoft Corporation. All rights reserved.

Try the new cross-platform PowerShell https://aka.ms/pscore6

PS F:\cypressSetup\cypress-test-techniques> npx cypress open
```

Once Cypress launched the app, choose the right browser and test to launch:

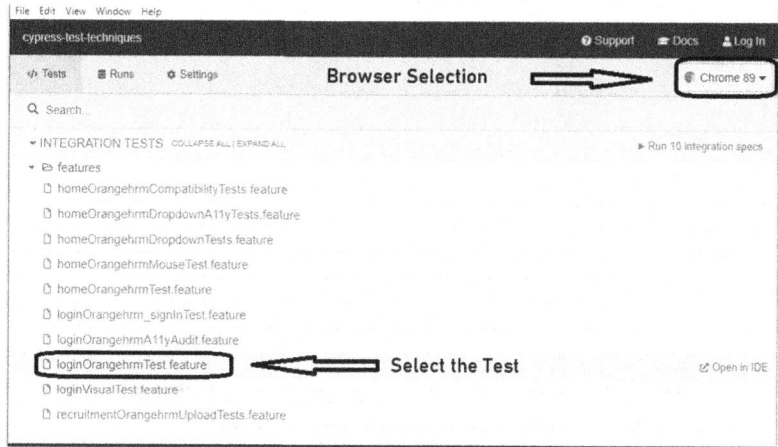

Picture: Cypress User Interface with the List of Tests.

Test Execution Without Thresholds on Lighthouse

It takes few seconds to load the tests since I use a old Windows operating system-based laptop (where as it is super fast in MacOS):

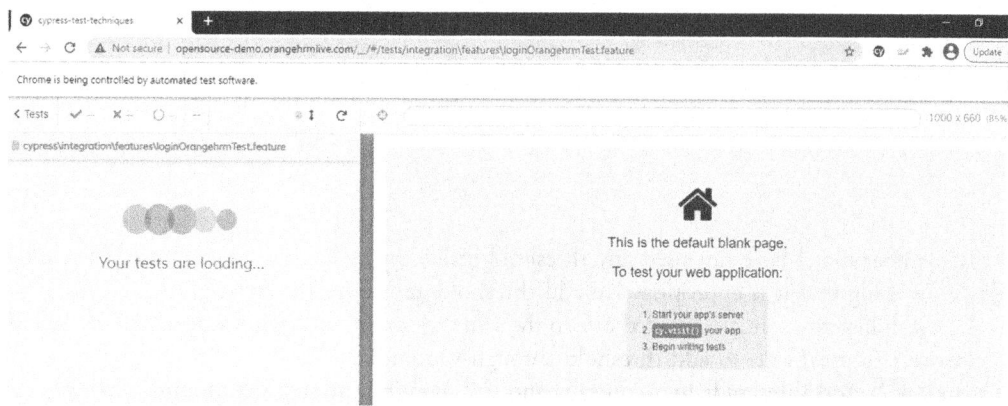

Picture: Cypress Test Execution that Controls the Browser for Website Interaction.

If you are new to CypressIO, you should know one major benefit of CypressIO is that it loads the browser and the website inside Cypress application itself. Where as the same website loaded in a browser through browser driver and the test instructions are sent as http protocol in open source tools, such as selenium, hence it takes huge time for interaction between selenium standalone, browser driver, browser, and website to interact. Hence it is a major win for CypressIO to control entire DOM elements to verify the website behavior.

On a different note, I was running the same site in different open source tool to check the speed of the webpage and the automation tool itself timed out waiting for the page to load most of the time; as a laugh or cry moment, I dropped the plan of continuing the script in that tool.

Key benefits of CypressIO tests are that it helps in running each step with more interactive playback and pause options at any point and rerun if I want to:

Picture: Cypress Launches the Website and Performs the Tests.

Unlike other steps, when Cypress runs the tests for cy.lighthouse command, it loads the same page in a new tab of the browser to start collecting the metrics:

Remember that I have not used any threshold inside my cy.lighthouse command, hence the tests show a log that it is appropriate to add threshold and rerun the tests:

In few milliseconds, my tests failed due to the same reason of not having a threshold to my test: Hence I stopped tests to add threshold through Option2.

Option 2: Add thresholds in a constant and call it inside the step definitions as below:

```
const lighthousemetrics = {
    performance: 95,
    accessibility: 100,
    "best-practices": 95,
    seo: 85,
    pwa: 100,
};

Then('I should see web audit results', function () {
    cy.lighthouse(lighthousemetrics);
})
```

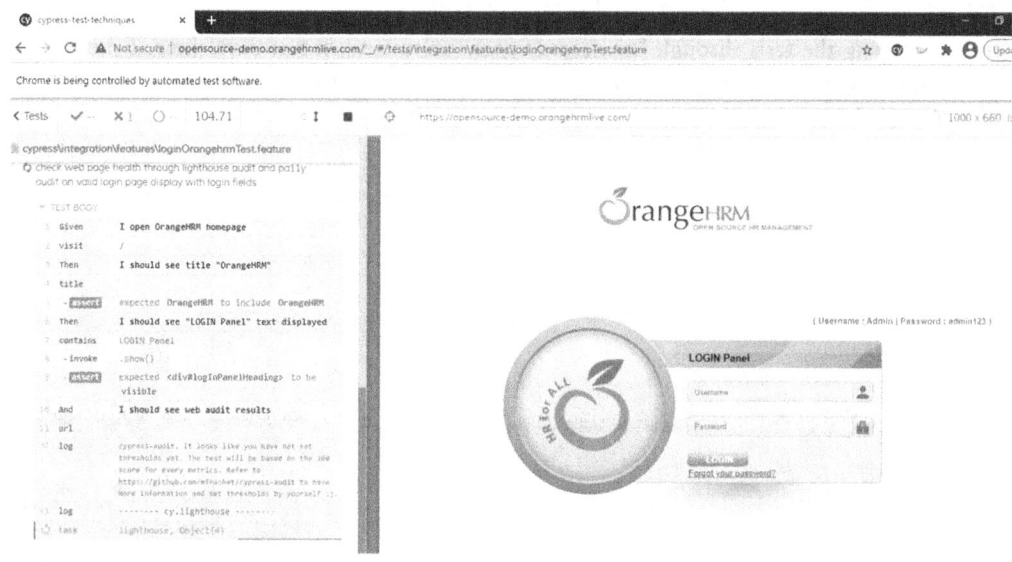

Picture: Cypress lIghthouse Commands Getting Executed on Run Time.

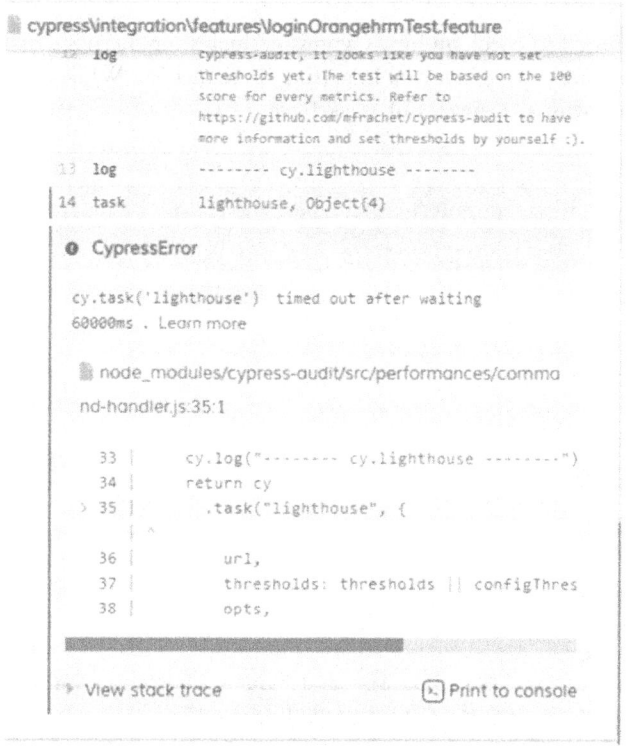

Picture: Cypress Lighthouse Timeouts.

Test Execution using Lighthouse Thresholds

While rerunning the tests through "*npx cypress open*" command, it not only showed the metrics after loading the page in a new tab and closed shortly, but also showed the path of the code in which the test failed due to the poor performance:

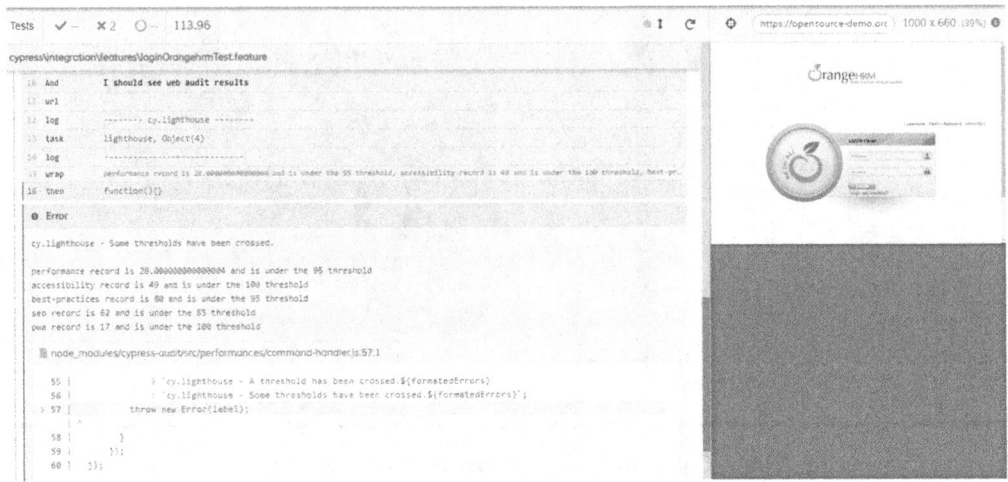

Picture: Cypress Lighthouse Display List of Results.

I was more interested to check on how Cypress evaluates the metrics dynamically on any web page and what components were involved in getting these metrics. While clicking on "view trace" it was even displayed with the metrics of stack trace:

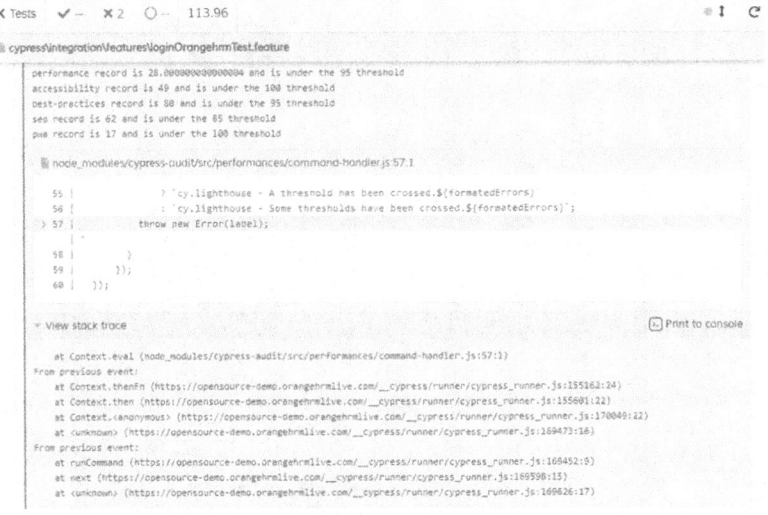

Picture: Cypress Lighthouse Displays the Detailed Errors List.

Test Execution Video

In Cypress.json, I have added two properties, such as

```
{
  "video": true,
  "videoCompression": 0,
}
```

These two lines helped me to record the test video and get it saved automatically under cypress \videos\ folder structure of the repository.

I used a command to run the tests in headless browser (Electron) using

```
npx cypress run --spec cypress\integration\features\loginOrangehrmTest.feature --browser chrome
```

Limitations

Execution Timeouts in Cypress v4

While running performance metrics tests using Cypress-audit-based lighthouse, it is possible to get the timeouts during the test run; this is due to the page load time and the interaction time between Cypress and the page response time. Hence, it is advisable to adjust retry configuration in cypress.json while running lighthouse related tests to retry again if the test failed first time. Alternatively it is advisable to install latest Cypress version, such as v7 to run the tests.

Cypress Videos

Cypress recorded videos are not always 100% compressed to include the steps of performance metrics assessment if the video is long.

Alternative Tool as Cypress-lighthouse

Cypress comes with a best in class plugin called Cypress-Lighthouse[1] in which plugin installation is made extremely simple with few steps:

Once Cypress framework has been setup, perform installation using the command below:

```
npm install cypress-lighthouse
```

Once installation is done through git bash or the terminal of the IDE, try adding the import command in the commands.js:

```
import 'cypress-lighthouse';
```

Once added, use the commands such as .lighthouse to verify your w

```
cy.lighthouse('https://www.orangehrm.com/').as('results')
```

Myth on Performance Metrics

When I asked on how to reduce this loading time to testers, I got surprising answers most of the time as "This is Non Functional Testing such as Performance Testing and not related to functional testing." As per my vast experience in software releases, this answer is 100% incorrect due to the reason that page load times are considered individual user experience and completely within the limits of functional testing; hence "performance metrics" to verify load time with single user and "performance tests" to verify load time with multiple users are two different test cases.

Hence performance metrics verification is the first priority test to be conducted within functional test cycles and it has been made compulsory from the pandemic times since most of us use websites during day to day activities. Finishing my article here without providing the fix strategies will be of no use for anyone to improve the performance metrics hence just raising the defect and not knowing where to fix the challenge will lead to long pending defects hiding somewhere in the backlogs to get hunted by scrum masters.

App Optimization and Chunking Fix Strategy

Let me take an example of a ReactJS application and show some useful fix mechanisms, such as app slicing and API response time improvements.

Most of the websites load very slow due to the loading time of dependent API calls, hence they are the first point of investigation to analyze and fix each API call to provide a better handshake between client and server. Once this is analyzed, immediate attention is needed for the app-mount file size. In other words, every ReactJS page loads fully when app.js file is loaded on the website with complete scripting. Most of the time this file will be served from cache after the first instance. Hence first time user will see some delays when comparing to a returned visitor to this website. Even after cache loading the page after first visit, app.js files should not weigh more than 5MB in worst case scenario. If the website is loading a file size of 3MB, that itself will cause some delay while loading the sites, hence chunking the files is the best way forward.

Increase the Requests and Maintain the Bundle

Use bunding tools like webpack or alternatives, such as browserify, almondjs, requires. It is better to separate the code written by developers and keep the code which is dependent to library or framework external to code and try caching the third-party code[2].

Try providing better experience to your website visitors first time and that will let them to become your repetitive customers without any additional efforts. But it may not be easy by just performing normal functional tests and traditional NFT tests. Cypress-audit and lighthouse has to be the best choice if you are trying to build a B2C website for large customer base.

This chapter of the book explained the Cypress plugins based-tests. But it did not explain the way to verify migrated tests from manual to automation, such as keyboard tests in which partial keyboard interactions can be potentially automated after running first time using screen readers as manual accessibility checks. Let us learn about those best practices in the next chapter.

Notes

1. Title: Cypress Lighthouse Plugin. (Accessed 12 December 2021). Retrieved from https://www.npmjs.com/package/cypress-lighthouse
2. Title: Code Chunking with Webpack—A pragmatic approach. (Accessed 12 December 2021). Retrieved from https://medium.com/react-weekly/code-chunking-with-webpack-a-pragmatic-approach-e17e8bcc6453

Chapter 21

Cypress Accessibility Testing using Keyboard Tests

Most of the testers think that they are using keyboards in day-in and day-out of their testing hence they do not need a dedicated test to perform "keyboard only" mode without mouse. Even though it seems like an idiotic idea when I discuss with friends and they end up laughing at me on "why I hate mouses-because will it bite me anytime?", but not many realize that one in five global population do not use mouse while accessing the websites, hence they need to get keyboard working for every other actions they perform on the websites. It may be few click away for us to book a cricket match ticket from popular ticket booking websites but it is not the same experience for those who can't see the screens due to their vision impairments. If you are still not convinced, please read WCAG guidelines 2.1.2, which states that any website developed for customers should not have any keyboard trap[1] and if they contain any form of keyboard traps, they are the potential severity 2 defects in your website to address it on priority since these are Level A defects. Please refer the open source test case repository on relevant test cases[2] to make sure that a dedicated test case covering the guidelines on WCAG 2.1.2.

Keyboard Only Tests are Crucial for Software Teams and Majority Misses It

According to my recent survey from LinkedIn, keyboard tests are crucial to QAs to include in their test scenarios and it is the same set of tests missed in majority of the organizations due to lack of clarity and purpose behind it. First of all, many QAs do not know what to do with "Keyboard Only Tests and Why?"; second, those who know the reasoning around accessibility are not aware on "how?"

Navigation Keystrokes: When QA aim to use keyboard shortcuts to navigate between the UI objects, the test step starts to count. Common keystrokes like "TAB" to navigate from top to bottom and "SHIFT+TAB" to navigate backwards would help to begin the tests.

Action Keystrokes: Press "Enter" in keyboard to activate links or buttons.

It is very simple to unplug the mouse from your laptop/desktop and give it to your cat to play whenever free.

DOI: 10.1201/9781003299431-23

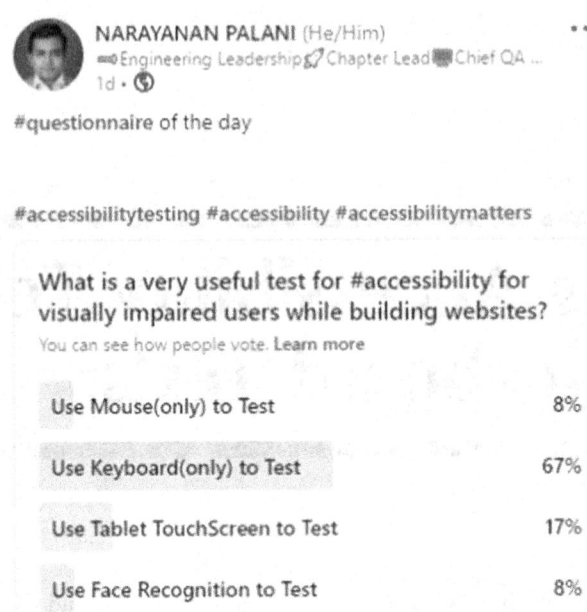

NARAYANAN PALANI (He/Him)
Engineering Leadership Chapter Lead Chief QA ...
1d ·

#questionnaire of the day

#accessibilitytesting #accessibility #accessibilitymatters

What is a very useful test for #accessibility for
visually impaired users while building websites?
You can see how people vote. Learn more

Use Mouse(only) to Test	8%
Use Keyboard(only) to Test	67%
Use Tablet TouchScreen to Test	17%
Use Face Recognition to Test	8%

Picture: Linkedin Survey on Keyboard Tests.

When to Perform Keyboard Automated Tests?

It is worth to perform manual accessibility tests soon after the page has been built by developers, hence automated keyboard tests need to be scripted exactly after the "manual screen reader accessibility tests" but before the end-to-end regression tests.

You may think on why these tests need an automation script in the first place, but it is highly possible that later defect fixes during regression test cycle may introduce a vulnerable bug called "keyboard trap." A keyboard trap occurs when a user can get into a field on a web page by using the keyboard but cannot get out of that field through the use of the keyboard or going in the circle of few fields continuously and not finding the way to come out of the loop. Developers not necessarily interested to introduce such defects but this can occur when defects getting fixes on the web pages in short time. In my experience, I have seen the keyboard traps when alerts or popup thrown on a web page and user is looped between the fields of background page but the page is grayed out and alert is displayed and user has no options to get the focus towards alert which is on the screen! Watch the example code at 28:27 from YouTube Video.[3]

Keyboard Tab to Navigate to Next Field

Install the plugin known as "cypress-plugin-tab"[4] to enable tab and shift-tab keyboard actions to use along with Cypress tests:

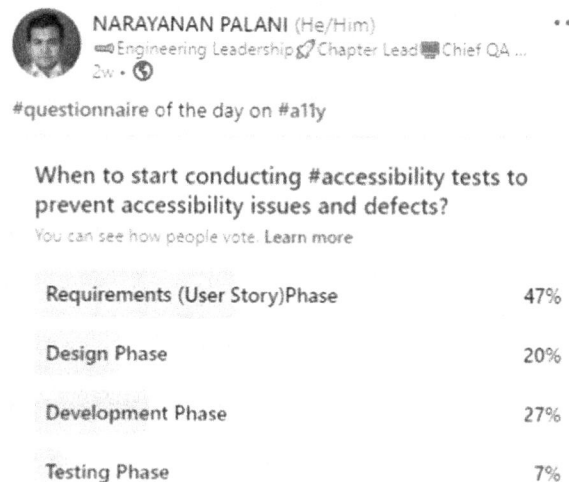

Picture: Linkedin Survey on Early Accessibility Testing.

npm install -D cypress-plugin-tab

Once installed, try using the require command at Cypress/support/index.js:

require('cypress-plugin-tab')

As a first level use case, I want to re-produce the customer behavior of TAB navigation from one field to next field in order to perform an action such as drop-down selection.

Feature: Dropdown functionality tests of home page using accessibility navigation

Scenario: Select sales manager job title in employees search list on PIM Tab using accessibility navigation
Given I open OrangeHRM homepage
When I SignIn as user
And I click on PIM tab of home page
And I navigate to jobtitle dropdown using keyboard functionality
And I click on dropdown of jobtitle
And I press enter on search button of pim tab
Then search results should be displayed successfully

Step Definition:

```
When('I navigate to jobtitle dropdown using keyboard functionality', () => {
  homeOrangehrmPage.navJobtitleusingKeyboard()
})
```

Function:

```
navJobtitleusingKeyboard () {
  cy.xpath(supervisorPIMtab).click().tab().focused(jobTitleDropdown_pim)
},
```

This test helps in navigating from previous field to dropdown field (target) using tab option from keyboard. If you carefully notice this function, I am focusing on a field prior to my actual target (dropdown field) and pressing Tab result in landing on to the dropdown field and I am checking that through "focused" to make sure that the dropdown field is focused.

Keyboard Shift Tab to Navigate backwards to a Field Prior to the Current Focus

Similar to tab() command, shift+tab can be implemented with the code as simple as .tab({shift: true})

Let us look at the sample code here.

Feature File:

```
    Scenario: Type employee name in employees search list on PIM Tab using accessibility
navigation-keyboard press shift tab
    Given I open OrangeHRM homepage
    When I SignIn as user
    And I click on PIM tab of home page
    And I navigate to employee name field using keyboard functionality
    And I enter the name Peter using keyboard
    And I press enter on search button of pim tab
    Then search results should be displayed successfully
```

Step Definition:

```
When('I navigate to employee name field using keyboard functionality', () => {
  homeOrangehrmPage.navempNameusingKeyboard()
})
```

```
When('I enter the name Peter using keyboard', () => {
  homeOrangehrmPage.enterempNameusingKeyboard()
})
```

Functions:

```
navempNameusingKeyboard () {
  cy.xpath(empIdPIMTab).click().tab({shift: true}).focused(empNamePIMTab)
},
enterempNameusingKeyboard () {
  cy.focused(empNamePIMTab).type('Peter')
},
```

After navigating to the employee name field backwards from employee id field using Shift+ Tab, typing the employee name as "Peter" helps in searching the employee list on the web page. This is more are like the same behavior of user when they don't use a mouse and try to navigate using keyboard and type the employee name to search and find.

It is also recommended to write one complete page's actions of Tab and Shift+Tab in one complete sequence to get checked. Alternatively, it can be scripted to verify newly introduced fields or components on the web page to check the nature of navigation on the web page.

Regular Keyboard Shortcuts to Test using Cypress

Majority of us use different keyboard operations[5] on the websites to perform different actions and these can be automated through Cypress and some of the same functions are provided here.

Useful Functions:

```
pressSearchusingKeyboard () {
  cy.xpath(searchBtn_pim).type('{enter}')
},

pressAltLeftusingKeyboard(){
  cy.xpath(pimTab_Homepage).type('{alt}{leftArrow}')

},
pressAltRightusingKeyboard(){
  cy.xpath(admin_tabxPath_Homepage).type('{alt}{rightArrow}')

},
pressAltRightusingKeyboard(){
  cy.xpath(admin_tabxPath_Homepage).type('{alt}{rightArrow}')
```

```
},
pressPageDownusingKeyboard(){
 cy.xpath(admin_tabxPath_Homepage).type('{pageDown}')
},
pressPageUpusingKeyboard(){
 cy.xpath(admin_tabxPath_Homepage).type('{pageUp}')
},
pressUpDownRightLeftusingKeyboard(){
 cy.get('body').type(
'{uparrow}{uparrow}{downarrow}{downarrow}{leftarrow}{rightarrow}{leftarrow}
{rightarrow}')
},
pressSelectAllusingKeyboard(){
 cy.xpath(admin_tabxPath_Homepage).type('{selectAll}')
},
pressMoveToEndusingKeyboard(){
 cy.xpath(admin_tabxPath_Homepage).type('{moveToEnd}')
},
```

Feature File:

Feature: Dropdown functionality tests of home page

Scenario: User navigate from PIM Tab to previous page by pressing ALT LEFT
 Given I open OrangeHRM homepage
 When I SignIn as user
 And I click on admin tab of home page
 And I use keyboard to navigate to go back to the previous page

Scenario: User navigate from Admin Tab to next page by pressing ALT RIGHT
 Given I open OrangeHRM homepage
 When I SignIn as user
 And I click on PIM tab of home page
 And I use keyboard to navigate to go to the next page

Scenario: User navigate from Admin Tab to next page by pressing ALT RIGHT
 Given I open OrangeHRM homepage
 When I SignIn as user
 And I click on PIM tab of home page
 And I use keyboard to navigate to go to the next page

Scenario: User perform page down from admin tab
 Given I open OrangeHRM homepage

When I SignIn as user
And I click on admin tab of home page
And I use keyboard to perform page down

Scenario: User perform page up from admin tab
Given I open OrangeHRM homepage
When I SignIn as user
And I click on admin tab of home page
And I use keyboard to perform page down
And I use keyboard to perform page up
And I use keyboard to perform multiple arrows from left right up down

Scenario: User perform SelectAll from admin tab
Given I open OrangeHRM homepage
When I SignIn as user
And I click on admin tab of home page
And I use keyboard to perform page down
And I use keyboard to perform select all

Step Definitions:

```
When('I use keyboard to navigate to go back to the previous page', () => {
  homeOrangehrmPage.pressAltLeftusingKeyboard()
})

When('I use keyboard to navigate to go to the next page', () => {
  homeOrangehrmPage.pressAltRightusingKeyboard()
})
When('I use keyboard to perform page up', () => {
  homeOrangehrmPage.pressPageUpusingKeyboard()
})
When('I use keyboard to perform page down', () => {
  homeOrangehrmPage.pressPageDownusingKeyboard()
})
When('I use keyboard to perform select all', () => {
  homeOrangehrmPage.pressSelectAllusingKeyboard()
})
When('I use keyboard to perform Move to End', () => {
  homeOrangehrmPage.pressMoveToEndusingKeyboard()
})
When('I use keyboard to perform multiple arrows from left right up down', () => {
  homeOrangehrmPage.pressUpDownRightLeftusingKeyboard()
})
```

Limitations with Cypress

Some keyboard shortcuts such as + are not available in Cypress at the moment. You may think why user would use that! Users use commands such as Ctrl+ "+" to perform "Zoom In" on any web page. Similarly, Ctrl+ "–" to perform "Zoom Out" and these are restrictions in Cypress since they are not yet supported until version 8.2.0. In addition, Cypress do not support "multi tab" tests as per Cypress Tradeoffs Website[6] hence performing "Ctrl+ PageUp" shortcut to move to previous tab and "Ctrl+ PageDown" shortcut to move to next tab are not in the scope of Cypress automated tests at the moment.

Available sequences in Cypress version 8.2.0 are: selectAll, moveToStart, moveToEnd, del, backspace, esc, enter, rightArrow, leftArrow, upArrow, downArrow, home, end, insert, pageUp, pageDown, {, alt, option, ctrl, control, meta, command, cmd, shift; if you want to skip parsing special character sequences and type the text exactly as written, pass the option: { parseSpecialCharSequences: false}

Are there No Alternatives to Mouse at All?

Not all users with disability use just keyboards and it is a misunderstanding in majority of the accessibility testers in current world. One set of users does not use mouse but some users with disabilities use mouse alternatives such as joysticks, track pad, track balls, etc. Hence testing with mouse is also another set of test to perform but it doesn't mean that "keyboard only" tests can be ignored.

NARAYANAN PALANI (He/Him) •••
Engineering Leadership Chapter Lead Chief QA ...
1w • Edited •

Most of the QAs.specific to #accessibility testing assumes that mouse should not be used for testing and keyboard is the only point of communication while interactive with websit ...see more

What are the mouse alternatives for the users with disabilities?

...see more

You can see how people vote. Learn more

LAPTOP TOUCHPAD	17%
JOYSTICKS.TRACK PAD.TRACKBALLS	38%
KEYBOARD WITH BUILT-IN MOUSE	29%
NO ALTERNATIVES AVAILABLE	17%

24 votes • Poll closed

Picture: LinkedIn Survey on Mouse Alternatives[7].

Do We Need to Run All Keyboard Tests Through Automation Test Scripts?

Not exactly right. It has to be tested using keyboard-based screen reader tests manually. It means, launching a screen reader along with running the scenarios through keyboard (without mouse) will get nice defects to be fixed. Once those items are fixed, it is better to automate and run them as part of regression Cypress pack, so that the defect fixes are not getting slipped in future code merges.

Summary on Keyboard Tests

While writing Cypress tests to mimic keyboard interactions, please make sure to read the copy on your website to make sure that the content is of simple language. Since the whole purpose of keyboard tests are to simply user behavior by using keyboards hence users with dementia (like Alzheimer's) may not pick up the meaning of complex English wordings (or any particular language's complex sentences). When a new developer joins in the team and introduces a small component of text box and collapses the complete order of the navigation, your "keyboard tests" are the only first hand tests to warn you on what went wrong in such keyboard issues. Otherwise it would have hours of manual keyboard accessibility tests to realize on what went wrong.

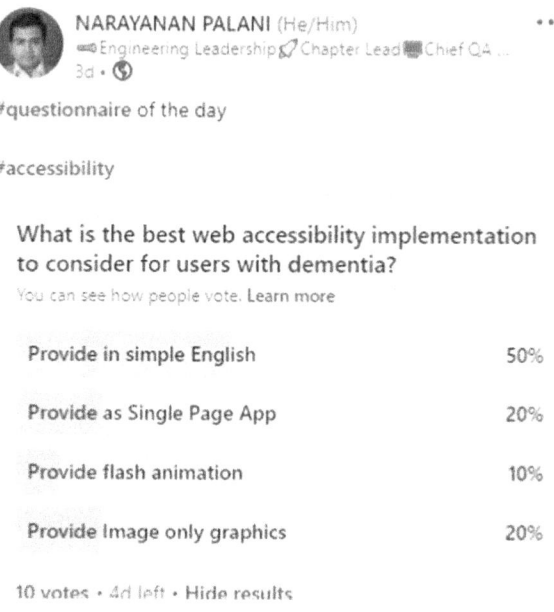

Picture: Linkedin Survey on Accessibility Implementation for Dementia Users.

Hence automating the keyboard navigations and thinking that the accessibility tests are completed are not the right approach. It needs to be reviewed time to time to make it a best experience for your customers.

We learnt about automating some keyboard interactions through automated Cypress tests so far. Let us learn about automating mouse interactions in Cypress tests in the next chapter.

Notes

1. Title: No Keyboard Trap:Understanding SC 2.1.2. (Accessed 12 December 2021). Retrieved from https://www.w3.org/TR/UNDERSTANDING-WCAG20/keyboard-operation-trapping.html
2. Title: Test Case from webAccessibilityTestCases/Operable. (Accessed 13 December 2021). Retrieved from https://github.com/narayananpalani/webAccessibilityTestCases/blob/master/Operable/WCAG_2.1.2_NoKeyboardTrap_Narayanan_Palani_TestCase_v1.xlsx
3. "[Code Demo] Focus Trapping in Modal System | JSer – Front-End Interview questions" YouTube video, (duration in 00:35:16), Posted by "JSer" (19 Mar 2021), video source: https://www.youtube.com/watch?v=hUlSgA8yrew
4. Title: Cypress-plugin-tab beta. (Accessed 12 December 2021). Retrieved from https://www.npmjs.com/package/cypress-plugin-tab
5. Title: Keyboard Shortcuts. (Accessed 12 December 2021). Retrieved from https://help.gnome.org/users/epiphany/stable/keyboard-shortcut.html.en
6. Title: Trade-offs. (Accessed 12 December 2021). Retrieved from https://docs.cypress.io/guides/references/trade-offs
7. Title: Linkedin Survey on Mouse Alternatives. (Accessed 12 December 2021). Retrieved from https://www.linkedin.com/posts/narayananpalani_accessibility-questionoftheday-activity-6826997409541853184-5uWk

Chapter 22

Cypress Accessibility Testing using Mouse Tests

Introduction

As many of us know, Cypress is one of the leading JavaScript test automation tools and it continues to introduce new innovative features to help developers and testers around the world to write tests in fastest way to verify the web apps. On the other hand, it is also one of the leading test automation tools that supports accessibility automation over html semantic element properties such as aria-label, etc.

Most of the QA engineers, specific to accessibility testing assumes that mouse should not be used for testing and keyboard is the only point of communication while interactive with websites to simulate the disabled user behaviors.

Even awareness of general public also not accurate and many are thinking that laptop touchpad can be accessible for most of the users with disabilities which is incorrect.

But there are good number of users worldwide with motor diseases who use mouse alternatives on their wheel chair setup to access the websites to perform day-to-day actions on web, such as joysticks, trackpad, track balls in day-to-day life. Still majority of the poll contributors mentioned that inbuilt keyboard mouse, laptop touchpad are the mouse alternatives for users with disabilities which clearly shows that the awareness yet to be made to QAs around the world.

Do read more on the mouse alternatives here: https://www.pretorianuk.com/mouse-alternatives

Hence manually testing all the mouse operations with mouse alternatives is extremely difficult for engineering teams in current world and we need a strong test automation solution to look at the mouse based test automation scripts.

While looking at the leading test automation tools such as selenium, the implementation is pretty hard with action.moveToelement() function to simulate the mouse behavior and it comes with huge amount of flakiness since the architecture of selenium is to interact from engine to browser driver and browser driver to browser that launched the website.

Based on my LinkedIn poll, I realized that majority of the QAs are still thinking that selenium is the only leading tool that helps in automating the mouse events:

DOI: 10.1201/9781003299431-24

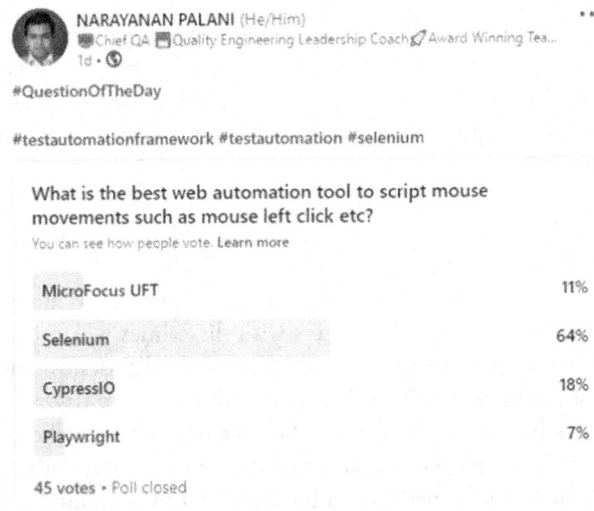

Picture: Linkedin Survey on Mouse Alternatives.

Picture: Linkedin Survey on Mouse Movement Tests.

This poll helps us with insights that not many QAs follow latest features of Cypress and it's features in automating mouse events. If you are reading this article, it is highly likely possible that learning Cypress-based mouse event automation will take your profile unique and strong when comparing to others who aware of just traditional scripting methods such as selenium[3].

Still I was not convinced to rely fully on manual mouse tests since the first hand "keyboard only accessibility tests" itself extremely time-consuming and unavoidable. So I chose to script and try it out in CypressIO.

Use Your Phone to Launch the Browser and Touch Start the Action on Your Website

When comparing the user behaviors 5 years ago, majority of the web users are from mobile-based traffic in current trends since desktop-based web users were heavily declined from Oct 2009 to Oct 2016 and mobile browser users crossed 51.3% traffic[4] from there on. After all, QAs are brought to represent the user behaviors to test and learn the defects before going live. So touchstart from mobile browsers are the first level tests which are missed by majority of the QA engineers while heavily relying on automated tests with the assumption that mouse behaviors wont produce any top severity defects. This is a complete myth.

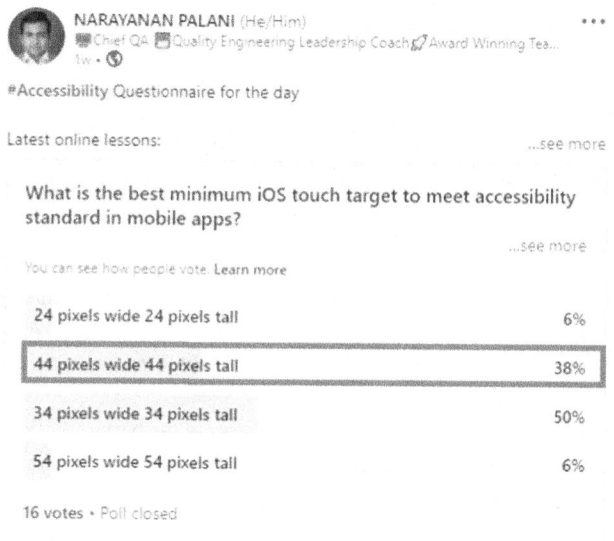

Picture: Linkedin Survey on iOS Touch Target.

Based on my recent poll in LinkedIn, I realized that most of the QAs don't know or not aware of the minimum required pixels for a touch target. It has to be minimum of 44 pixels wide and 44 pixels tall (according to WCAG guidelines 2.5.5 Target Size[5]) but only 38% of my poll contributors selected right. This proves that the awareness is not made wide across testing space and this will definitely lead to defect leaks across touch targets when users use the web or app interactions in their mobile phones.

"Unresponsive Touch Screen" is a most occurred defect in majority of the mobile devices when interacting with mobile browsers. This is usually common when the server facing huge load and trying to facilitate the delayed page load. If you are thinking that your selenium tests are going to cover this behavior, you need to simulate that API delays by setting up hard wait times in API configurations in order to run your selenium tests. But do you know if that is still a right solution?

You may think that what is that the man with laptop doing in the image provided above, when this chapter talks about touchstart functions, right? These days, quality engineers use their virtual mobile devices through perfecto, headspin, or saucelabs-based providers to interact with websites to see mobile browser behaviors hence it is highly likely possible that you may encountered similar experiences to test those browser mouse incompatibility defects in the past.

Function written to call the trigger option from Cypress in order to touch start on a tab:

```
touchAdminTab () {
  cy.xpath(admin_tabxPath_Homepage)
    .invoke('show')
    .should('be.visible')
    .trigger('touchstart')
},
```

Step Definition:

```
When('I move touchstart using mouse on admin tab section', () => {
  homeOrangehrmPage.touchAdminTab()
})
```

With these few lines of code, I have been reproducing the same behavior of mobile browser touchstart in my script. Now you may think that how on earth I have run this test on a mobile (challenge no. 1) and how did I manage to get the API delayed response without downgrading my API infrastructure? (challenge no. 2)

If I am using CypressIO, I don't need to worry about both the challenges to be honest.

But I had a second thought and asked a group of 10,000+ engineers on LinkedIn to figure out what are their awareness on minimum touch space to perform touch start.

How to Resolve Challenges in Test Automation Code to Run the Mobile Browser Tests with Cypress Tests?

All I need to do is to launch the browser and reload the page with respective viewport of particular mobile or tablet version I wanted to test against. Entire viewport combinations ranging different iPhone versions, macbook versions, iPad versions, and popular Android versions are listed in Cypress documentation.[6]

After reloading the page with particular viewport, I just need to perform the trigger event to perform mobile interactions, such as touchstart.

Feature File:

```
Feature: MouseEvents verification in various compatibility models of devices

Scenario: Mouseactions on Dashboard Tab Graph using iPhone6 Mobile
    Given I open OrangeHRM homepage
    When I SignIn as user
    When I see the page in iphone6 version
```

When I perform move actions on dashboard graph
Then text insights displayed below dashboard successfully

Scenario: Mouseactions on Dashboard Tab Graph using iPhonexr Mobile
Given I open OrangeHRM homepage
When I SignIn as user
When I see the page in iphonexr version
When I perform move actions on dashboard graph
Then text insights displayed below dashboard successfully

Scenario: Mouseactions on Dashboard Tab Graph using macbook-15 device
Given I open OrangeHRM homepage
When I SignIn as user
When I see the page in macbook-15 version
When I perform move actions on dashboard graph
Then text insights displayed below dashboard successfully

Scenario: Mouseactions on Dashboard Tab Graph using iPad2 device
Given I open OrangeHRM homepage
When I SignIn as user
When I see the page in iPad2 version
When I perform move actions on dashboard graph
Then text insights displayed below dashboard successfully

Step Definition to launch or reload the page with Iphone6 viewport:

```
When('I see the page in iphone6 version', () => {
  homeOrangehrmPage.viewPortIphone6()
})
```

Function:

```
viewPortIphone6 () {
  cy.viewport('iphone-6')
},
```

Step Definition to launch or reload the page with IphoneXR viewport:

```
When('I see the page in iphonexr version', () => {
  homeOrangehrmPage.viewPortIphonexr()
})
```

Function:

```
viewPortIphonexr () {
  cy.viewport('iphone-xr')
},
```

Step Definition to launch or reload the page with macbook-15 viewport:

```
When('I see the page in macbook-15 version', () => {
  homeOrangehrmPage.viewPortmac15()
})
```

Function:

```
viewPortmac15 () {
  cy.viewport('macbook-15')
},
```

Step Definition to launch or reload the page with iPad2 viewport:

```
When('I see the page in iPad2 version', () => {
  homeOrangehrmPage.viewPortipad2()
})
```

Function:

```
viewPortipad2 () {
  cy.viewport('ipad-2')
},
```

How to Simulate the Throttle Time or Delays in the Page Load?

"URL Throttler"[7] Chrome extension is a simple answer to this question. If are you launching the tests in "npx cypress open" mode, just need to add this plugin and rerun the tests. If you are thinking that the tests are immediately getting the Cypress browsers closed when tests are getting over and you are unable to add plugin on the fly, of course you need to run the tests with suffix "--no-exit" to avoid exit after tests finished running all steps.

Mouse Events using Cypress

Desktop/laptop-based mouse events are the key behaviors to get automated and verified time to time in order to understand how new defects leaked in such complex mouse events such as down, up, leave, left, and right, etc.

Recently, I have been searching for a better test automation solution to automate the mouse tests since the bad mouse behaviors impacting the business when websites are not reacting to user's click actions on time. Especially odd mouse behaviors, touch interactions, and failure interactions through mouse are high in Internet Explorer versions of web browsers. On the other hand, users with disabilities are heavily depend on mouse alternatives such as joysticks, trackballs, track pad, and switch interface devices which perform similar click actions like actual mouse devices.

Mouse Down Events using Cypress

Mouse interactions such as mouse down and up are helpful to change the UI display behaviors to help users with easy dynamic interactions.

Sample code[8]:

```
<!DOCTYPE html>
<html>
<body>

<p id="qaSelectorMouseUpDown" onmousedown="mouseDown()" onmouseup="mouseUp()">
Click the text! The mouseDown() function is triggered when the mouse button is pressed
down over this paragraph, and sets the color of the text to yellow. The mouseUp() function
is triggered when the mouse button is released, and sets the color of the text to green.
</p>
<script>
function mouseDown() {
document.getElementById("qaSelectorMouseUpDown").style.color = "yellow";
}
function mouseUp() {
document.getElementById("qaSelectorMouseUpDown").style.color = "green";
}
</script>
</body>
</html>
```

If these mouse events needed scripts from Cypress, it can be done with just one liner. That's true.
Step Definition:

```
When('I move mouse down on admin tab section', () => {
  homeOrangehrmPage.mousedownAdminTab()
})
```

Function:

```
mousedownAdminTab () {
  cy.xpath(admin_tabxPath_Homepage)
    .invoke('show')
    .should('be.visible')
    .trigger('mousedown')
},
```

Mouse Over Tests with CypressIO

Mouse Over is a common user interaction to navigate toward a web component using mouse to hover over[9] to understand the particular section.

These mouse over interactions can be easily scripted with .trigger('mouseover') tests:

Step Definition:

```
When('I move mouseover using mouse on admin tab section', () => {
  homeOrangehrmPage.mouseoverAdminTab()
})
```

Function:

```
mouseoverAdminTab () {
  cy.xpath(admin_tabxPath_Homepage)
    .invoke('show')
    .should('be.visible')
    .trigger('mouseover')
},
```

Step Definition:

```
When('I mouseover on first row of results table of admin tab', () => {
  homeOrangehrmPage.mouseOverAdminResultTableR1C2()
})
```

Function:

```
mouseOverAdminResultTableR1C2 () {
  cy.xpath(admin_resultTableRow1Column2)
    .invoke('show')
    .should('be.visible')
```

```
      .trigger('mouseover')
},
```

Step Definition:

```
When('I mouseover on second row of results table of admin tab', () => {
  homeOrangehrmPage.mouseOverAdminResultTableR2C2()
})
```

Function:

```
mouseOverAdminResultTableR2C2 () {
  cy.xpath(admin_resultTableRow2Column2)
    .invoke('show')
    .should('be.visible')
    .trigger('mouseover')
},
```

Mouse Leave Tests with CypressIO

Once mouse over event[10] is performed, mouse leave event helps in going back to the earlier stage of the UI display and find the script to simulate the same behavior through CypressIO:
Step Definition:

```
When('I mouseleave on first row of results table of admin tab', () => {
  homeOrangehrmPage.mouseleaveAdminResultTableR1C2()
})
```

Function:

```
mouseleaveAdminResultTableR1C2 () {
  cy.xpath(admin_resultTableRow1Column2)
    .invoke('show')
    .should('be.visible')
    .trigger('mouseleave')
},
```

Mouse Move Events with CypressIO

Automating Move events through CypressIO are helpful when navigating from one section of the page to another section of the page to monitor the co-ordinates and those mouse moves[11]-based tests help reduce the manual accessibility tests in greater percentage when automated.

Function to perform mouse left and mouse right events:

```
mousActionsonDashboardGraph () {
  cy.xpath(graph_dashboard)
  .as('graph')
  .trigger('mousedown')
  .trigger('mousemove')
  .trigger('mouseup')
  .trigger('mouseleft', { which: 1, pageX: 600, pageY: 100 })
  .trigger('mouseright', { which: 1, pageX: 600, pageY: 600 })
  .trigger('mouseleave')
},
```

Now let us look at the complete feature file which shows the scenarios together.
Feature File:

```
Feature: Home Page Mouse Movement Test on OrangeHRM website

  Scenario: Right Click on Admin Tab of home page
    Given I open OrangeHRM homepage
    When I SignIn as user
    And I click on admin tab of home page
    And I move mouse down on admin tab section
    Then the Admin tab should be displayed

  Scenario: Touch start on Admin Tab of home page
    Given I open OrangeHRM homepage
    When I SignIn as user
    And I click on admin tab of home page
    And I move touchstart using mouse on admin tab section
    Then the Admin tab should be displayed

  Scenario: Mouseover on Admin Tab Results of home page
    Given I open OrangeHRM homepage
    When I SignIn as user
    And I click on admin tab of home page
    And I mouseover on first row of results table of admin tab
    And I mouseover on second row of results table of admin tab
    Then the Admin tab should be displayed
```

Scenario: Mouseleave on Admin Tab Results of home page
   Given I open OrangeHRM homepage
   When I SignIn as user
   And I click on admin tab of home page
   And I mouseover on first row of results table of admin tab
   And I mouseleave on first row of results table of admin tab
   Then the Admin tab should be displayed

Scenario: Mouseactions on Dashboard Tab Graph
   Given I open OrangeHRM homepage
   When I SignIn as user
   When I perform move actions on dashboard graph
   Then text insights displayed below dashboard successfully

Automating mouse events and touch start interactions not only reduces the workload but also facilitates helping find more defects when small code changes being made in the complex development code repository. Since it is difficult to perform mouse interactions every time through manual tests, automated mouse tests and getting them run through Cypress–Jenkins integrated tests are smarter way to spot defects.

We learnt on both keyboard and mouse-based automated accessibility tests in the last few sections. But what to use when User Interface has got misalignments and how to capture such defects when text boxes or buttons not placed at right location? These are captured through visual tests. Our last chapter talks about visual tests in detail. But we need to understand on why these visual tests are part of accessibility. The answer is simple. When users are having partial eye impairment, they get announced about a particular button on the website and assume that the button is misaligned and kept at bottom left of the website due to an alignment defect. In such case, users with partial vision impairment will get confused on finding the button on time. Similarly, if the user is hearing impaired and trying to find a button to submit the form but the submit button hidden as a result of misalignment—this will cause confusion when trying to submit the forms, hence visual tests are pretty much part of the accessibility test coverage.

Notes

1. Title: Cities4allcampaign Linkedin Post from Victor Santiago Pineda. (Accessed 12 December 2021). Retrieved from https://www.linkedin.com/posts/victorpineda_cities4allcampaign-worldenabled-cities4all-activity-6875150410282348544-KtLd
2. Title: World Enabled: removing barriers and promoting access with cities around the world. (Accessed 12 December 2021). Retrieved from https://vimeo.com/432304929
3. Title: How to perform mouseover function in Selenium WebDriver using Java? (Accessed 12 December 2021). Retrieved from https://stackoverflow.com/questions/17293914/how-to-perform-mouseover-function-in-selenium-webdriver-using-java
4. Title: StatCounter Global Stats. (Accessed 12 December 2021). Retrieved from https://techcrunch.com/wp-content/uploads/2016/11/internet_usage_2009_2016_ww.png?_ga=2.76295516.894542909.1627686225-1461687580.1627157052

5. Title: Understanding Success Criterion 2.5.5: Target Size. (Accessed 12 December 2021). Retrieved from https://www.w3.org/WAI/WCAG21/Understanding/target-size.html
6. Title: Arguments. (Accessed 12 December 2021). Retrieved from https://docs.cypress.io/api/commands/viewport#Arguments
7. Title: URL Throttler. (Accessed 12 December 2021). Retrieved from https://chrome.google.com/webstore/detail/url-throttler/kpkeghonflnkockcnaegmphgdldfnden?hl=en
8. Title: On Mouse Down. (Accessed 12 December 2021). Retrieved from https://www.w3schools.com/jsref/tryit.asp?filename=tryjsref_onmousedown
9. Title: On Mouse Over. (Accessed 12 December 2021). Retrieved from https://www.w3schools.com/jsref/tryit.asp?filename=tryjsref_onmouseover
10. Title: On Mouse Enter. (Accessed 12 December 2021). Retrieved from https://www.w3schools.com/jsref/tryit.asp?filename=tryjsref_onmouseenter
11. Title: On Mouse Move. (Accessed 12 December 2021). Retrieved from https://www.w3schools.com/jsref/tryit.asp?filename=tryjsref_onmousemove

Chapter 23

Summary

Web Accessibility, a basic need to verify accessibility of every website, is no longer an optional test or is not considered as a low priority Non Functional Tests (NFT) in many organizations. Even though accessibility, security, and performance were originally counted as NFT tests, accessibility is a feature's inbuilt attribute to support user interactions to give better web experience for users with difference disabilities. Hence it is a primary top priority functional test when developing web application as per my industry experience in the past decade. 15% of C-Suite leaders state that it's hard to secure a budget for digital accessibility according to recent survey results[1]. So making your company, an accessibility focused organization is a better way to tell your vision to whole staffs and co-workers to start making the changes to include digital accessibility.

Changing the focus from "Automation First Approach" to "Accessibility First Approach" is essential and this change is required at every organization to start focusing on better future for their customers who have different set of disabilities.

We discussed about different accessibility best practices in "web accessibility project" with illusionary user personas to learn tips and tricks around page title, language, heading, landmarks, links, navigation, table, list, page break, drag and drop, images, user entry (redundant entry) and single page applications-based web accessibility. In the second half of the book, Cypress-based test automation techniques are discussed across plugins, such as cypress-audit, cypress-axe, cypress-image-snapshot, and cypress-visual-regression. Huge efforts were taken in creating the open source repository on "Web Accessibility Test Cases,"[2] hence requested readers need to clone the test cases and refer to write new test cases for your own web accessibility projects.

Detailed Cypress-based test automation techniques are discussed in my earlier book on "Automation Software Testing with Cypress"[3] and similar accessibility automated test implementation on selenium testing tools are discussed in "Advanced Selenium Web Accessibility Testing."[4]

Thank you for taking part in Web Accessibility Project, a wonderful journey on learning tips and techniques to make the web world accessible for users. As accessibility evangelists, let us take a pledge to improve our software projects, websites, and deliverables better accessible and adhering to accessibility guidelines to give a wonderful experience to next-generation customers.

Now that you have finished reading "The Web Accessibility Project," you are faced with a mission critical choice: start to make digital accessibility a deep part of your application development or do nothing and experience zero digital transformation.

DOI: 10.1201/9781003299431-25

Need Your Support

If you have been inspired by the models, frameworks, and concepts discussed in the book "The Web Accessibility Project" and want to help others awaken their accessibility awareness, here are some action steps you can take immediately to contribute to the better future:

- Share your book selfie, write thoughts about this book on social media sites. You can blog about this book and provide a book review with stars.
- If you are a manager or lead in software projects, you can invest in copies of this book so all of your engineers, colleagues can lead the way to improve web accessibility.
- Gift the book "The Web Accessibility Project" to co-workers, job seekers, university students, and family members. They will learn that they are meant to make a better future with strong support to digital accessibility.

Recommended Readings

An engineer from Web Accessibility Project usually spends 30 minutes to 1 hour everyday in learning the latest developments of accessibility best practices. Hence keeping eyes and ears wide open is crucial to thrive and implement latest tricks of web development. Let us look at some of the niche sources of information to learn everyday.

Part A: Manual Web Accessibility Development and Testing

Introduction and Scope

Accessibility Fundamentals. (Accessed 13 December 2021). Retrieved from https://docs.microsoft.com/en-us/learn/paths/accessibility-fundamentals/

Digital Accessibility Resources. (Accessed 13 December 2021). Retrieved from https://www.essentialaccessibility.com/resources

Digital Accessibility 101. (Accessed 13 December 2021). Retrieved from https://www.levelaccess.com/resources/webinar-digital-accessibility-101/

Webinars: Using Assistive Technology (AT) in Accessibility Testing. (Accessed 12 December 2021). Retrieved from https://www.accessibilityassociation.org/s/archived-webinar-details?id=a0A3p000014 wdFJEAY

Keyboard and Mouse Alternatives and Adaptations. (Accessed 13 December 2021). Retrieved from https://abilitynet.org.uk/factsheets/keyboard-and-mouse-alternatives-and-adaptations

Screen Magnification. (Accessed 13 December 2021). Retrieved from
https://abilitynet.org.uk/factsheets/screen-magnification

Web Accessibility Basics and Accessibility Failure Models

Learn the Basics of Web Accessibility. (Accessed 13 December 2021). Retrieved from
https://docs.microsoft.com/en-us/learn/modules/web-development-101-accessibility/

Tackling a Huge Website with WCAG-EM. (Accessed 12 December 2021). Retrieved from
https://www.accessibilityassociation.org/s/archived-webinar-details?id=a0A3p000014wd
VKEAY

GEL Technical Documentation: Guidance for Developers Building Accessible Websites
based on BBC GEL (Accessed 13 December 2021). Retrieved from
https://bbc.github.io/gel/

User Personas of Web Accessibility Project

Agile Accessibility in a Regulated Industry. (Accessed 12 December 2021). Retrieved from
https://www.accessibilityassociation.org/s/archived-webinar-details?id=a0A3p000014wd
RkEAI

Session6 of Free Training Series: Web Accessibility for Product and Marketing Teams.
(Accessed 13 December 2021). Retrieved from
https://www.levelaccess.com/resources/web-accessibility-training-product-and-
marketing/

WAVE Accessibility Evaluation Tool

WAVE Help. (Accessed 13 December 2021). Retrieved from
https://wave.webaim.org/help

Website Page Title based Accessibility Development

Testing Walkthrough. (Accessed 13 December 2021). Retrieved from
https://digitalaccessibility.uoregon.edu/assessment/testing

Website Language based Accessibility Development

Language Identification. (Accessed 13 December 2021). Retrieved from
https://digitalaccessibility.uoregon.edu/guidelines/language

Website Landmarks based Accessibility Development

> DOM Order Matters. (Accessed 13 December 2021). Retrieved from
> https://developers.google.com/web/fundamentals/accessibility/focus/dom-order-matters

Website Headings based Accessibility Development

> Headings. (Accessed 13 December 2021). Retrieved from
> https://digitalaccessibility.uoregon.edu/guidelines/headings

Website Links based Accessibility Development

> Using tabindex. (Accessed 13 December 2021). Retrieved from
> https://developers.google.com/web/fundamentals/accessibility/focus/using-tabindex

> Introduction to Focus. (Accessed 13 December 2021). Retrieved from
> https://developers.google.com/web/fundamentals/accessibility/focus

Website Navigation based Accessibility Development

> Semantics and Navigating Content. (Accessed 13 December 2021). Retrieved from
> https://developers.google.com/web/fundamentals/accessibility/semantics-builtin/
> navigating-content

Website Tables based Accessibility Development

> Tables. (Accessed 13 December 2021). Retrieved from
> https://digitalaccessibility.uoregon.edu/guidelines/tables

Website Lists based Accessibility Development

> Quick Tips for Writing Meaningful Alt Text (Even If You're Not a Writer). (Accessed
> 13 December 2021). Retrieved from
> https://www.levelaccess.com/resources/quick-tips-writing-meaningful-alt-text-even-
> youre-not-writer/

Website Page Media – Page Break based Accessibility Development

> Page Break Navigation (2.4.13 – Level A). (Accessed 13 December 2021). Retrieved from
> https://www.wuhcag.com/page-break-navigation/

Single Page Application based Accessibility Development

> Recommendations for Single Page Applications. (Accessed 13 December 2021).
> Retrieved from
> https://a11y-guidelines.orange.com/en/articles/single-page-app/

Website Redundant Entry based Accessibility Development

> 7 Quick Facts about WCAG 2.2. (Accessed 13 December 2021). Retrieved from https://www.levelaccess.com/7-quick-facts-about-wcag-2-2-2/

Website Drag and Drop Functionality based Accessibility Development

> Accessible Drag and Drop – Why Foolproof Scripting Is Critical When Using ARIA. (Accessed 13 December 2021). Retrieved from https://www.levelaccess.com/accessible-drag-and-drop-why-foolproof-scripting-is-critical-when-using-aria/

Website Images based Accessibility Development

> Bringing CSS and SVG Back into the Accessibility Spotlight. (Accessed 12 December 2021). Retrieved from https://www.accessibilityassociation.org/s/archived-webinar-details?id=a0A3p000014wdR0EAI

Part B: Automated Web Accessibility Development and Testing

Cypress JavaScript Test Automation Framework Setup

> Cypress YouTube Videos. (Accessed 13 December 2021). Retrieved from https://www.youtube.com/c/Cypressio/videos

> Cypress Automation Testing. (Accessed 13 December 2021). Retrieved from https://engineers-hub.teachable.com/p/cypressio

Cypress Accessibility Testing using Cypress-Audit

> Test Automation for Accessibility from Test Automation Universiry. (Author: Marie Drake) (Accessed 13 December 2021). Retrieved from https://testautomationu.applitools.com/accessibility-testing-tutorial/

Cypress Performance Metrics and Accessibility Score

> Tools for Web Developers-Lighthouse. (Accessed 13 December 2021). Retrieved from https://developers.google.com/web/tools/lighthouse

Cypress Accessibility Testing using Keyboard Tests

> Cypress Type Arguments. (Accessed 13 December 2021). Retrieved from https://docs.cypress.io/api/commands/type#Arguments

Keyboard and Mouse Alternatives and Adaptations. (Accessed 13 December 2021). Retrieved from https://abilitynet.org.uk/factsheets/keyboard-and-mouse-alternatives-and-adaptations

Cypress Accessibility Testing using Mouse Tests

Cypress Trigger. (Accessed 13 December 2021). Retrieved from https://docs.cypress.io/api/commands/trigger

Keyboard and Mouse Alternatives and Adaptations. (Accessed 13 December 2021). Retrieved from https://abilitynet.org.uk/factsheets/keyboard-and-mouse-alternatives-and-adaptations

Cypress Accessibility Testing using Visual Tests

Automated Visual Testing with WebDriverIO from Test Automation University. (Author: Nyran Moodie). (Accessed 13 December 2021). Retrieved from https://testautomationu.applitools.com/automated-visual-testing-javascript-webdriverio/

Session3 of Free Training Series: Web Accessibility for Product and Marketing Teams. (Accessed 13 December 2021). Retrieved from https://www.levelaccess.com/resources/web-accessibility-training-product-and-marketing/

Useful Webinars, Podcasts And Universities

AbilityNet Webinars. (Accessed 13 December 2021). Retrieved from https://abilitynet.org.uk/free-resources/webinars

Deque Accessibility Webinars. (Accessed 13 December 2021). Retrieved from https://www.deque.com/resources/type/webinars/

United in Accessibility Podcast. (Accessed 12 December 2021). Retrieved from https://www.accessibilityassociation.org/s/podcast

Access University. (Accessed 13 December 2021). Retrieved from https://www.levelaccess.com/solutions/training/access-university/

Deque Digital Accessibility Courses & Accessibility Reference Lib. (Accessed 13 December 2021). Retrieved from https://dequeuniversity.com/

Notes

1. Title: What do C-Suite leaders think about digital accessibility? (Accessed 12 December 2021). Retrieved from https://abilitynet.org.uk/news-blogs/what-do-c-suite-leaders-think-about-digital-accessibility

2. Title: webAccessibilityTestCases. (Accessed 12 December 2021). Retrieved from https://github.com/narayananpalani/webAccessibilityTestCases

3. Title: Automated Software Testing with Cypress 1st Edition. (Accessed 12 December 2021). Retrieved from https://www.amazon.com/gp/product/0367699540/ref=dbs_a_def_rwt_hsch_vapi_tpbk_p1_i1

4. Title: Advanced Selenium Web Accessibility Testing: Software Automation Testing Secrets Revealed. (Accessed 12 December 2021). Retrieved from https://www.amazon.com/gp/product/1949449432/ref=dbs_a_def_rwt_hsch_vapi_tpbk_p1_i0

Index

Printed in the United States
by Baker & Taylor Publisher Services